*Routledge Revivals*

# The Role of the Pupil

Although the role of the teacher has been extensively explored, the role of the pupil has received very little attention in the sociology of education. This authoritative study, *The Role of the Pupil* (first published in 1975), is about what it means to be a school pupil, exposed to the often-conflicting expectations of teachers, parents and peers.

The author has drawn on a wide range of sociological literature to focus not only on the basic role of pupil as learner but also on other important but neglected facets of the pupil role. The pupil appears as child-to-be-socialised, as teacher's adversary, as savage-to-be-civilised, as customer, as wrong-doer. These viewpoints provide a fresh perspective on pupil relationships within and beyond the classroom. This book will be of interest to students and researchers of education and sociology.

# The Role of the Pupil

Barbara Calvert

Routledge
Taylor & Francis Group

First published in 1975
by Routledge & Kegan Paul Ltd
This edition first published in 2024 by Routledge
4 Park Square, Milton Park, Abingdon, Oxon, OX14 4RN

and by Routledge
605 Third Avenue, New York, NY 10017

*Routledge is an imprint of the Taylor & Francis Group, an informa business*

© Barbara Calvert 1975

**Publisher's Note**
The publisher has gone to great lengths to ensure the quality of this reprint but points out that some imperfections in the original copies may be apparent.

**Disclaimer**
The publisher has made every effort to trace copyright holders and welcomes correspondence from those they have been unable to contact.

A Library of Congress record exists under LCCN: 75319492

ISBN: 978-1-032-86038-1 (hbk)
ISBN: 978-1-003-52099-3 (ebk)
ISBN: 978-1-032-86040-4 (pbk)

Book DOI 10.4324/9781003520993

# The Role of the Pupil

## Barbara Calvert

*Senior Lecturer in Education*
*University of Otago, New Zealand*

ROUTLEDGE & KEGAN PAUL
LONDON AND BOSTON

First published in 1975
by Routledge & Kegan Paul Ltd
Broadway House, 68-74 Carter Lane,
London EC4V 5EL and
9 Park Street,
Boston, Mass. 02108, USA
Set in Linotype Pilgrim
and printed in Great Britain by
Northumberland Press Ltd, Gateshead

ISBN 0 7100 8065 4 (c)
0 7100 8066 2 (p)

THE STUDENTS LIBRARY OF EDUCATION has been designed to meet the needs of students of Education at Colleges of Education, and at University Institutes and Departments. It will also be valuable for practising teachers and educationists. The series takes full account of the latest developments in teacher-training and of new methods and approaches in education. Separate volumes will provide authoritative and up-to-date accounts of the topics within the major fields of sociology, philosophy and history of education, educational psychology, and method. Care has been taken that specialist topics are treated lucidly and usefully for the non-specialist reader. Altogether, the Students Library of Education will provide a comprehensive introduction and guide to anyone concerned with the study of education, and with educational theory and practice.

In recent years sociologically inclined writers have produced a great deal on the role of the teacher, the role of the head and administrative roles. Selection, equality, the curriculum and classroom relations have all come under the sociological microscope. But next to nothing has been written about pupils as pupils. In this book Barbara Calvert draws upon a wide range of sociological literature to focus attention on the pupil role, and in so doing helps to throw fresh light on the tasks that teachers face in classroom and school. Her book will be of value to students and experienced teachers alike.

WILLIAM TAYLOR

# Contents

4 Candidates for salvation                              32
  *Reforming zeal*                                      32
  *Candidates for reform*                               34
  *The pupil looks ahead*                               36
  *Conclusion*                                          37

5 Natural enemies                                       38
  *Pupils hide their shortcomings*                      39
  *Pupils defy their teachers*                          39
  *Resentment of authority*                             40
  *Ritual expression of hostility*                      42
  *Backstage behaviour*                                 44
  *Pupils with something to hide*                       45
  *Constructive aspects of conflict*                    47
  *Summary*                                             49

6 Customers and clients                                 50
  *Ways of making choices*                              51
  *Buying education*                                    53
  *Choosing at preschool and university levels*         54
  *The teachers' claim to know best*                    54
  *Being 'hooked' on school*                            55
  *'Free play' and pupil choice*                        56
  *Choice and commitment*                               58
  *Guidance and counselling*                            59
  *Conclusion*                                          61

7 The factory and the garden                            62
  *Quality control*                                     64
  *Human rejects*                                       65
  *The school as a garden*                              66
  *Conclusion*                                          67

8 Pupils amongst their peers                            68
  *The school sets the stage*                           69
  *Playground games*                                    70

ix

CONTENTS

# 1

# A neglected role

You tell us that you fail only the stupid and the lazy. Then
you claim that God causes the stupid and the lazy to be
born in the houses of the poor. But God would never spite
the poor in this way. More likely, the spiteful one is you
(Barbiana, 1970).

This extract is taken from one of the very few statements in
which pupils have set down their own idea of what it means
to be a pupil. It is to be found in a remarkable book called
*Letter to a Teacher*, in which a group of Italian schoolboys
aged eleven to thirteen, drop-outs from the state school
system, address themselves passionately to the teachers who
have let them down.

It is rare for pupils to present their views of what it is
like to be a pupil. It is comparatively rare for anyone else,
either, to discuss the role of the pupil. In this book I have
tried to make a coherent statement about the ways in which
pupils are expected or 'supposed' to behave. I have set out
not so much to list the expectations which govern pupil
behaviour, but rather to examine the kinds of expectations
that exist, the reasons for their existence, and the consequences.

*Who learns?*

Education is supposed to be *for* the pupil; that is, the primary benefit from participation in the educational process is supposed to accrue to the pupil, and not to the teacher or the administrator or any other person or group in society. And in so far as society as a whole expects to gain, this is supposed to happen principally through gains achieved by the pupil. We might expect, therefore, that in the study of education there would be more emphasis on learning than on teaching; learning is the important happening and teaching exists to promote learning. Moreover the pupil may learn without the teacher teaching, but the teacher cannot be said to have taught if the pupil does not learn. In fact, Illich (1971) claims that it is a major illusion of the school system that most learning is the result of teaching.

The psychology of education does in fact give a central place to learning, but in the sociology of education the activities of the teacher have received much more attention than those of the pupil. Much has been written about the role of the teacher but the role of the pupil has largely been ignored. This is the more surprising when we reflect that the central activities prescribed by both roles – teacher and pupil – take place in the common arena of the classroom, so that each role depends for its satisfactory performance on the interlocking performance of the other role. Ultimately it would seem more logical for the teacher's role to depend on the role of the pupil than vice versa, but logic is not the key to the formulation of roles.

*A neglected perspective*

Why, then, have sociologists tended to neglect the role of the pupil? Presumably it is not because they see teaching as essentially more important than learning. Statements of educational aims such as appear in suggestions to teachers,

2

school prospectuses and political party platforms correctly focus on the pupil as the principal beneficiary of the education system, and even teachers' unions often cite the pupils' interest as the main reason for improving the conditions under which teachers work. But, politically, every other group concerned with education – teachers, administrators, planners, parents, employers and society at large – can obtain a better hearing for its own point of view than can the pupil. In particular, teachers as a group are highly articulate and well able to voice their concern over their own role.

Even political pressures, however, might not by themselves constrain sociologists of education to focus so much on the teacher's role were it not that the writings of educationists are produced largely for an audience of teachers. For this audience the problems of teachers are a major preoccupation, and it is natural to concentrate on the teacher's role and the conflicts associated with that role. Even this book, which proposes to focus on the role of the pupil, is written not for pupils but for teachers and for others who share their interests, and the material is thus selected as in some way relevant to those interests.

There is indeed a sense in which the pupil has less need to be concerned over his role than the teacher. The teacher's position is based on an occupational choice: the teacher prefers teaching over the other occupational alternatives currently open to him, is in some degree committed to his work, and is paid to engage in that work. The pupil's position, on the other hand, is (for most of the inmates of our schools) a matter in which he has no choice. He occupies that position by virtue of his age. Nobody pays him to perform satisfactorily, although he may be promised rewards in the distant future. In some cases he may remain uncommitted to his role, and manage to retain his self-esteem while failing as a pupil. Lacey (1970), for instance, relates a pupil's claim that out-of-school knowledge is far more important than school knowledge: this pupil knew far more than his

3

teacher about stocks and shares. The importance of a good performance of the pupil role is also implicitly challenged by all those adults who years later boast of their stupidity and wickedness at school. So the pupil may be able to insulate himself against the worst effects of failure by claiming that what he does at school is unimportant; but the teacher cannot make this claim, and consequently successful performance of his role is more important to the teacher. This in turn could lead to a greater concern for the role of the teacher in educational writings.

But perhaps the most important reason for the neglect of the pupil's role is to be found in the fact that the pupil's position is among the disvalued positions of our society. Like the position of the child, and the position of the patient, it lacks status; it commands little respect. Behaviour appropriate to a disvalued position tends to be defined for the occupants of that position by those who occupy related positions of greater status: the role of the child is defined by the adult, the role of the patient by the doctor or nurse, and the role of the pupil by the teacher. The teacher as it were writes the lines and directs the performance of the pupil.

Because the teacher thus defines the pupil role, he tends to see himself as the more decisive participant in the performance, and thinks of the pupil's role as more receptive than his own. Things are done by the teacher to or for the pupil, just as things are done by the doctor to or for his patient; and the pupil, like the patient, is expected to conform to the expectations thus set up for him.

Yet the accepted view of learning as essentially an activity of the learner seems to require a view of the learner's role as involving something more than meeting the teacher's expectations, something that does or should incorporate the expectations – and hopes and aspirations – of the pupil himself. This in itself suggests that it is worthwhile to study carefully the role of the pupil.

4

## Constituents of the pupil role

Of course roles always exist as part of a complex set of inter-relationships between people in different positions. The pupil is a member of a cast involving teachers, parents and others. The relationship between pupil and teacher is a principal relationship for both pupil and teacher, and when we describe the role of the teacher in this relationship we describe by implication the role of the pupil in the same relationship. But in practice the complexities of social interaction may prevent us from getting the teacher and pupil roles into simultaneous focus; and besides, there are important segments of both teacher's and pupil's role which are played out in separate settings. Therefore any specification of pupil role derived solely from a consideration of the teacher-pupil relationship would be incomplete. The pupil, for instance, enters into relationships with his peers, corresponding to but not much resembling those of the teacher with his colleagues; and the pupil's role in relation to his parents is quite different from the role of the teacher in relation to the same parents. Thus many elements of the pupil's role have no counterpart in the role of the teacher.

For these reasons, then, it is useful to try to interpret the life of the school in terms of the role of the pupil. As the central figure in the educational drama the pupil has a role which deserves more attention than it usually gets.

But we cannot exactly adopt the standpoint of the pupil. Although we have all stood in the place where a child stands, we have since then stood in so many other places that we can no longer see things just as they looked to us as children. Still less can we see things as they look to children today growing up in a very different world from that of our own childhood. Anyway, our reasons for wanting to understand the child's point of view are our own adult reasons. We want to understand so that we may interact with the child in the way that will produce the outcomes we most desire. Hence

5

we seek not a child's-eye view but simply a greater understanding of the way the world presses in on the child, of the
requirements laid on him or perceived by him in his position
as a pupil.

## What we mean by a pupil's 'role'

It is appropriate at this point to consider precisely what we
mean when we speak of a pupil's *role*. We mean a set of
expectations people have for the behaviour of the pupils.
Actual behaviour often conforms to these expectations and
sometimes does not conform. To distinguish between the
expectations and the behaviour it is convenient to refer to
role-behaviour.

If it is to be meaningful to discuss the role of the pupil,
there must be a degree of consensus amongst people about
how they expect a pupil to behave. In fact, there must be
some consensus about what pupils do, if we are to make use
of the concept of 'pupil' at all. This consensus is far from
perfect. The expectations for pupil behaviour will vary somewhat depending on whether we consult teachers, parents,
the pupils themselves, or some other group. They will also
vary amongst teachers in different schools, and even perhaps
amongst teachers in a single school. But a school could not
function unless teachers, and pupils and parents too, had some
common expectations about when the pupils should be there,
where in the school they should be, what the teachers are to
ask them to do, how they are to respond to their teachers,
and a host of other matters. Variations in expectations give
rise to possibilities of conflict in pupils, and the concept of
role-conflict is a useful one for trying to understand pupils'
behaviour.

In describing a role as made up of *expectations* for
behaviour we must clarify a further point. We are talking
about what people are 'supposed' to do because they occupy
a stated position, the position of pupil, or teacher, or parent,

6

or prefect. We are not referring to what we *anticipate* they will do. Thus pupils may be 'expected' or 'supposed' to report to the headteacher if they are not going straight home after school, and yet the headteacher may not really anticipate that they will do so; and if they suddenly began conforming to the rule chaos might result. Conversely the headteacher may anticipate that a certain number of pupils will travel to school by bus, but there is no requirement or expectation laid on them to do this. Because of the confusion that may arise from the use of a word like 'expectations', which is ambiguous in common use, sociologists often use the word 'norm' to cover all kinds of do's and don'ts for behaviour, such as laws, rules and regulations, customs, etiquette and good taste, and on occasion also the beliefs and attitudes it is appropriate for people in a particular position to hold. For instance, various kinds of norms require a pupil to attend school regularly, to be on time, to respect his teacher, not to tell tales, to want to pass examinations, to disapprove of cheating, and not to eat in class.

## Looking for information about the pupil role

What sources of information are available for the study of the role of the pupil?

It would be useful to draw on both empirical studies of the expectations held by pupils, teachers and others for pupil behaviour in a variety of settings, and theoretical analyses of underlying assumptions and of relationships between expectations. However, studies of either sort are rare. Expectations for teacher behaviour have been explored by asking teachers, student teachers, other students, head-teachers, school administrators, pupils and parents about the behaviour and attributes they expect or approve of or like from teachers, and the conflict experienced by teachers in meeting these expectations has been studied, but no parallel sources of information are available about pupil behaviour.

7

Nevertheless a great deal can be inferred from other sources.

In the first place, because the most important relationship associated with the roles of both teacher and pupil is their relationship with each other, all the behaviours expected for teachers in this relationship imply reciprocal expectations for pupils, and these we can try to tease out.

Further, role theory in general suggests some lines of attack on the analysis of pupil roles. It leads us, for instance, to consider the likely influence of the other positions which pupils may occupy, on their roles as pupils. They are sons or daughters, newspaper boys, Girl Guides, shoppers, club members, and all of these involve roles which could impinge on, shape or interfere with their roles as pupils. And within the pupil role itself there are possibilities of conflict as there are within the teacher role.

Besides empirical studies of expectations relating to teachers, and deductions based on role theory, we can also take account of a large body of educational literature that has indirect implications for pupil roles. As an example, here is a letter written by a teacher to a parent, quoted in a case study of a boy who had been progressing poorly at school but had improved (Rothney, 1968):

> Dear Mrs . . .,
> Bruce is doing good work in reading and average work in all other subjects. If he can learn to control his habit of talking out of turn, he can be a good citizen and an asset to the group.
> > Miss . . .

This letter clearly implies numerous expectations about making progress, talking, citizenship and integration into the group, and about the part to be played by pupil, parent and teacher in bringing about improvement. By implication, part of the pupil's role is to develop self-control, to work hard, to do some talking but not too much, and to respond to the efforts of the teacher to help and change him.

8

Then again, statements in school prospectuses, curriculum goals and official regulations offer possible source materials. Even educational tests throw light on certain behavioural expectations imposed by the testers and often shared by the pupils.

Most of the time actual behaviour reflects the expectations that people have for behaviour, and this means that we can study the expectations by looking at what actually goes on. Especially if it goes on without occasioning surprise or disapproval or embarrassment, we can assume that observed behaviour is in accordance with role prescriptions.

Thus we could examine reports of observers in schools, such as the books by Hargreaves (1967) and Lacey (1970). In similar vein the Opies (1969) have described common playground games, and their study throws light on pupil peer group norms. A further refinement of observers' reports is the use of video-tapes to capture behaviour as it happens and preserve it for detailed analysis. This has been done in researches such as those of Adams (Campbell, 1970).

Besides factual reports there are numerous works of fiction and autobiographical accounts of school life which can be turned to account as a source of insights into the norms governing pupil behaviour in various times and places. Some well-known examples are *Tom Brown's Schooldays* (Hughes, 1948 ed.), *Stalky and Co.* (Kipling, 1929), *Roaring Boys* (Blishen, 1966) and *To Sir, With Love* (Braithwaite, 1961).

Thus there is no shortage of material which could be sifted to accumulate indirect evidence about the role of the pupil, but little use has been made of the material by students of education. In the following chapters a number of these sources will be used as a basis for the description of pupil roles or to illustrate propositions about these roles.

We shall begin our exploration, since the pupils we are going to consider are mainly children, by looking at the role of the child. Of course in its widest sense the term 'pupil' refers to anyone who is being taught, regardless of age or context. But we shall concentrate rather more narrowly on those who are taught in schools, especially primary schools and secondary schools. After considering the role of the child, we shall study selected aspects of the typical pupil role, and some less typical variants, both approved and disapproved. Then follows a brief account of role conflict as it affects the role of the pupil, and a discussion of ways in which the role is changing.

# 2
# The child role

In modern societies a 'school' is so often an institution for the education of the young that we tend to think of a pupil as a child. Yet even in modern societies there are many schools for adults. And, in mediaeval societies where monasteries were the principal schools, pupils were commonly adults. The growth of adult education in our own time, coupled with incipient revolt against upward extension of secondary education, may bring us again to a period when there are so many adult pupils that the role of the pupil is no longer closely linked with childhood.

Meanwhile the distinction between child pupil and adult pupil is reflected in the use in Britain of the term 'student' to refer to the adult or near-adult pupil. In the United States on the other hand it is common to find the term 'student' applied to school children as well as adults.

Our present concern is essentially with pupils at primary and secondary schools, and since these pupils are children it is useful to examine the child role as a source of some of our expectations for the behaviour of pupils.

## Children are immature

To be a child is to be small, weak, ignorant, incapable and to lack power and status in comparison with adults. Because children are inferior to adults in these ways they are expected to defer to the superior knowledge, skill and judgment of adults. They are to believe what adults tell them, to obey orders from adults, and to refrain from certain activities requiring skill (like driving a car). They are to accept the moral values prescribed by adults.

At the same time their lapses are often tolerated or overlooked. They are given a certain amount of licence to behave irresponsibly or at least to invoke their youth in extenuation of irresponsible behaviour. A broken window may be excused with the remark, 'boys will be boys'. A troublesome prank may be put down to mere youthful exuberance. The legal system deals differently with offences committed by children under a stated age, holding them less responsible for their acts and giving them some immunity from punishment.

### Children are not responsible

The origins of children's behaviour are variously conceived by adults. Some adults see children as essentially wicked or mischievous, always ready to 'get away with' unacceptable behaviour if not suppressed. In the eyes of other adults children are essentially innocent, devoid of malice and incapable of doing wrong by their own fault; if they offend they are victims of poor heredity or a poor environment.

### Children lack status

Children are seen as less important than adults. They should give priority to adults when seats are scarce, should join in conversations only when adults want them to, and their preferences should not weigh as heavily as those of adults when decisions are to be made about such matters as interior decoration or holidays. It is true that families do exist in which life revolves round the desires of the children, but this state of affairs is frowned on by the majority of adults, and

12

parents in such families are at pains to justify their indulgence of their children by reiterating that 'after all they are only young once'. Children's activities are similarly less important than adults' activities. They are expected to spend a great deal of time playing, and indeed to 'go away and play' whenever adults want to be busy. But children's play is so unimportant that it is to be laid aside at a moment's notice whenever an adult wants the child's time.

### Children are delicate

While children's concerns are considered less important than the affairs of adults, children are nevertheless seen as more easily damaged than adults. This is an additional reason for not allowing them to do what they like. Children's behaviour is to be governed more than adult behaviour by what is 'good' for them – they must not smoke, drink (at least on the same scale as adults), eat a great deal of rich food, stay up late, or wear fashionable shoes. Adults should see that children get what is good for them, whether or not it is what the children want.

And, again because they are more easily damaged, children are to be shielded from physical hardship or from emotional trauma. Many were sent to safe places during World War II. They are to be protected from disturbing knowledge of family rows, impending family breakup, illness or death.

### All our future

In the last resort when survival is at stake children take priority over adults. For scarce space in a lifeboat, or for scarce supplies of food, they have first claim, for the future of the race is with them.

*Children are dependent on adults*

As a baby the human being depends on others for the meeting of all his needs, and this is a biologically given fact which limits the ways in which we can treat little children. As children grow older their role changes. The behaviour expected of toddlers differs conspicuously from that expected from children of primary school age, and this in turn is quite unlike that expected from teenagers.

Teenagers are expected to anticipate adult status by acting responsibly, thus showing themselves fit to be trusted – but they are expected to act in this way without being in fact trusted. Independence is proffered inconsistently and unevenly. They may be called in the morning when it is time to get up, and they may have their clothes washed, ironed and mended for them – things they are physically quite capable of doing for themselves. Yet they may be expected to take responsibility for their study habits and manage their sexual relationships with assurance – things that many adults cannot accomplish.

When adolescents leave school and start work their roles change literally overnight. They are expected or allowed to assume an adult role while their contemporaries who remain at school continue to perform an immature role. There would be a good argument for reversing these expectations and allowing senior secondary school pupils more freedom than early leavers, since the pupils who stay longest at school are potentially more mature and capable for their age than those who leave early. Adolescents who marry and become parents are likewise accorded adult status while their age-mates are still treated as immature.

*An ambiguous role*

The clarity of the child role seems to diminish as children grow from babyhood to adolescence. Parents, and adults

14

generally, are usually quite clear about their duty to care for and protect young babies even when they are not sure about the best way to do this. At the toddler stage there is still consensus in our culture (even if not between our culture and other cultures) that children should be encouraged to achieve independence in eating and toilet training and dressing as soon as possible. From this time on, the drive by adults to establish independence in the young slows down, and by the time adolescence is reached we are often trying to prevent children from assuming independence rather than encouraging them to spread their wings. We try to limit their spending power, their choice of clothes, and their right to make decisions about education and work and leisure.

The result is a great deal of confusion in the minds of both children and parents about what is expected of children as they approach adulthood. Even apart from general confusion about what is expected, parents often find it hard to change their roles as their children grow up, and tend to treat their sons and daughters as though they are younger and less competent than is actually the case.

To add further to the confusion, the expectations parents have for children's behaviour change with successive children in a family. The first child is usually under far greater pressure to achieve well in and out of school than later children, he is helped and encouraged more, and he is also more restricted in his choice of friends and his freedom to go out. As families come to have fewer children, the overall proportion of children who have to meet the expectations for the oldest increases, and there are proportionately fewer with the kind of freedom that younger children in a large family achieve. The early children in a family have inexperienced parents, the later ones have experienced parents. The more small families there are, the fewer children have experienced parents.

*Cultural components of the child role*

Ivan Illich (1971) is one writer with outspoken views about childhood, which he regards as a construct of modern society:

> We have grown accustomed to children. We have decided that they should go to school, do as they are told, and have neither income nor families of their own. We expect them to know their place and behave like children.... We are expected to tolerate the childish behaviour of children.

Illich claims that the 'mass production of childhood' became possible 'only with the advent of industrial society', and this childhood is produced through the school system. He sees the role of the child as a burden which the child would gladly avoid if he could, but the role is unfortunately perpetuated because children are by definition pupils, and pupils are needed to provide 'an unlimited market for accredited teachers'.

While this considerably distorts the facts, Illich is right both in linking the child role with the pupil role, and in pointing out that at least some of the supposed characteristics of children are constructs of our own society, disseminated through our institutions and especially through the school, which has a vested interest in its own image of childhood. If we do not accept Illich's analysis as applicable to early and middle childhood, at least it is hard to escape the conclusion that our culture has invented adolescence and invested it with qualities which are in part arbitrary.

It is interesting to set Illich's view of the cultural origin of the child role beside findings in cross-cultural studies. In an interesting study of the behaviour of mothers towards their children in six different cultures (Minturn and Lambert, 1964), support was obtained for several hypotheses which link aspects of the child role with social conditions in a particular society. For instance, it was found that children were more severely punished for fighting with each other when many

16

people must share cramped living quarters yet still retain their friendship. The authors considered that their evidence generally supported the view that child-rearing practices are rooted in environmental pressures:

> Most studies in this area have approached socializing practices as if the parents of the investigations were operating in terms of blue-prints and curriculums that are guided largely by either cognitively-monitored theories about what is good and bad for the long range development of children, or at the other extreme, molded by the parents' own unconscious motives and anxieties, which translate themselves into behaviour and, in turn, mold the children's psyches without the parents' knowledge or control.

> It now appears that the pressures impinging upon the growing child are much more in the nature of by-products of the horde of apparently irrelevant considerations that impinge on the parents ... of household composition, size of family, work load, etc.

Whiting (1963), reporting an earlier section of the same study, concluded that child-training practices are based on 'conditions in the natural and social environment' that make them necessary for survival, and the practices are then rationalised and justified by a structure of beliefs and values designed to support them.

Changes in the 'conditions in the natural and social environment' could, if we agree with Whiting, be expected to change first the behaviour we expect from children and then the reasons we give for our expectations. For instance, because we live in a more affluent society than that of our parents, we may be able to give our children fruit juice and a choice of prepared cereals for breakfast, instead of porridge. We may then use theories about the vitamin content of fruit juice, and the dangers of forcing children to eat something they don't like, to justify abandoning the porridge.

Although children are generally considered less competent

than adults, there is one thing they are supposed in our culture to be able to do better than adults. They are supposed to have a special facility for learning things, which adults lack. 'You can't teach an old dog new tricks.' Consequently formal learning has high priority in children's lives while adults are commonly excused from further formal learning.

## The age basis of the child role

The role of the child is assigned largely on the basis of age, although we often extend the age boundaries in the case of mentally handicapped people. Because of the age basis for the classification of individuals as children, anomalies occur when children are advanced or retarded for their age. Consider the case of a five-year-old who on his first day at school pointed to a map on the wall and asked if it was a map of Australia. 'Yes,' said the teacher, 'How did you know?' 'It's written on it,' was the scornful retort. This child was not as ignorant as five-year-olds are supposed to be, and he had no need of the pre-reading and reading programmes the school was geared to provide for its five-year-olds. Probably he and his teacher were both going to be frustrated by his inability to perform the normal five-year-old role. Although this is an extreme instance, it was common a few years ago for teachers to discourage parents from teaching children to read or even allowing them to learn to read before they reached school age. There are some things children are not supposed to know until they are taught them by the official agency.

The age basis for classification leads to anomalies also in our expectations for problems of adjustment. Children because of their youth are not only allowed but expected to have adjustment problems from time to time. Adults because of their greater age are expected, in the literature on dealing with children's problems, to be both free of problems themselves and able to help children solve their problems. These role prescriptions ignore or implicitly deny the emotional

18

maturity of some children and the emotional immaturity of some adults. When special institutions like schools are set up in a society, catégorisation of some sort is inevitable, and some people are inappropriately assigned to roles which do not suit their needs or capacities. Some children who do not need to learn what the school tries to teach are required to be pupils, and some adults who need or wish to learn these things are excluded.

*Inconsistencies in the child role*

Our discussion shows that there are many contradictions and ambiguities in our ideas about the role of the child. Children are important and unimportant; they are expected to behave childishly but criticised for this childishness; they are supposed to play with absorption when they are told to play, and not to mind stopping when they are told to stop; they are supposed to be responsible when it suits adults and to be dependent when adults prefer dependence; they are supposed to think for themselves, but they are criticised for original solutions to problems. Such inconsistencies are, of course, to be found in any social role. They complicate the task of learning the rules – but they also preserve us in some measure from the dangers of consistent adherence to a single principle. Consistency could reduce the available repertoire of role behaviours and the ease of adaptation to changing circumstances. There is the danger that 'one good custom should corrupt the world'.

In spite of the inconsistencies, there is widespread consensus about a few guiding principles for the behaviour of children. We have discussed the general inferiority and dependence of children. Underlying the low status resulting from this position there is, however, a general belief in the tremendous importance of children. They are the adults of the future, and this requires the investment of a great deal of the community's resources to prepare them for that future.

They are expected to devote a large part of their time and energy to acquiring the knowledge, skills and attitudes they will need later as adults. This pursuit is expected to take precedence over their present pleasures and their play.

## Preparation for adult life

The view of childhood as a time of preparation for adulthood is a striking feature of our culture, and it has very great educational significance. It results in the provision of schools which the child is compelled to attend. Schooling as a whole is seen as a preparation for adult life, and each stage of schooling is seen as a preparation for the stage beyond. Even preschool education is seen by many as first and foremost a preparation for school. 'They could at least learn to sit still and listen,' complains a mother criticising a free play programme. And Mason (1967) asks wistfully about adolescence, 'Is it to be a time of life when all is waiting, and nothing doing?' According to the norms of our society it is just that. There was a time when the whole of life was regarded as a preparation for a life beyond. This view has lost ground in our time, but the idea that fulfilment for the child is to be found in a life beyond childhood is still very much in evidence. 'When you grow up you can decide for yourself.' 'When you have a house of your own you can do what you like.'

There is nevertheless some evidence of a changing view of the function of childhood. The Ministry of Education report, *Half our Future* (Newsom Report, 1963), refers in several places to the right of the school child to day-by-day pleasure : 'There has to be room for simple enjoyment.' This right has been generally conceded by educationists and parents in the case of preschool children. At the stage of primary education, the concept of 'play-way' has gained a hold, and attempts are made to combine enjoyment for the child with learning for future use. At the post-primary level, on the other hand, the pupil's right to enjoy his school life is slower to gain

20

support, but many would at least on reflection agree with Kelley (1962) when he wrote, 'The secondary school simply must be a good place for all youth, because there is no other place in our society for them'; and Kelley's idea of a good place was not a place devoted first and foremost to gaining qualifications for the future.

The future is far away for children. Even for adults a future several years away often seems remote. On the child's time scale his own adulthood must seem so remote as to be scarcely real, so if he is to defer gratification now in favour of some future good, he will do so because we insist, and not because he prefers the future good. Small wonder that many children lack commitment to the goals adults have for them.

## Conclusion

Whatever view a community takes of the role of its children, the school is expected to establish a pupil role that will be compatible with the child role. In summary, there are great variations in the detail of the child role, but in general children are expected to occupy a subordinate position. Their dependence on adults is to be maintained at a suitable level, and their behaviour regulated so as to cause the minimum of disruption to adult society; and their activities are to be regulated by their future roles especially as workers. The school is supposed to enforce behaviour which accords with these prescriptions.

# 3

# Discipline and instruction

Because the role of the pupil is enacted largely as a counter-part of the teacher's role, in the classroom or in some other teacher-dominated setting, we can learn about the pupil's role indirectly by studying the role of the teacher in these settings. It will be convenient to begin our exploration of the pupil role by examining the most important features of the role of the teacher, since a considerable volume of writing has appeared on this topic.

Recent writers agree in identifying the two principal components of the teacher's role as discipline and instruction. Hargreaves (1972) considers that these are the two basic sub-roles. Hoyle (1969), Musgrove and Taylor (1969) and many other writers also emphasise one or both of these two sub-roles, and there seems to be considerable unanimity amongst teachers, pupils and parents that they are basic requirements.

Many other aspects of the teacher-pupil relationship receive mention : the teacher also reforms, sets an example to, be-friends, leads, helps, cultivates and entertains his pupils, and promotes their 'self-actualisation'. These other activities are, however, less central to the teacher's role than discipline and instruction, at least in typical school settings.

## Controlling pupils

Of these two central concerns, discipline perhaps has first place, at least for teachers in training and teachers at the outset of their school careers. Student teachers show their concern for their role as disciplinarians through the value they place on practice teaching and their demand for instruction in teaching techniques. From practice and techniques they hope to acquire control, and in the anxious quest for control they often find educational philosophy, history, sociology and even psychology somewhat irrelevant. The problems of beginning teachers with control are recorded in novels written by teachers (Braithwaite, 1961 and Blishen, 1966, for instance). Instruction, although it is the central goal of teaching, implies order as a prerequisite.

If the teacher's first concern is to establish order, this implies that the first requirement for the pupil is that he submit to the teacher's authority. This fits very well with cultural norms for the role of the child.

## The place of routines

Requirements imposed on pupils in the effort to establish control may include arrangements for assembling and entering the classroom or moving from room to room or to the playground and back in a quiet and orderly way; standing and sitting at prescribed times (as standing to address a teacher or when the headteacher enters); refraining from talking or moving about the classroom without permission; engaging in prescribed work; and waiting quietly for instructions. Work has to be done in the right book, with the right headings, margins and spacings, at the right speed; and the right (that is, the taught) methods of solving problems must be used. Specified procedures must be followed for handing in work and receiving it back. All these arrangements set the stage for the actual instruction, and also demonstrate the authority of

23

the teacher. In proportion as many acts have been integrated into set routines, the teacher and pupils are freed to concentrate on non-routine aspects of situations, including new material to be learnt.

Set routines vary from school to school, so that new pupils (and new teachers) take some time to become familiar with the school's expectations. Even terminology may change, so that what was called English in the pupil's last school is known in his new school as Literature and Comprehension, or as Language and Communication.

Not only are there variations between schools, but individual classrooms have their own versions of some parts of the routines. Miss Roberts expects her class to rise to their feet and chant 'Good morning, Miss Roberts' when she enters the room, while Mrs Fletcher expects that her pupils will already have their books out and will continue quietly with their work. Some uniformity will be imposed on the school as a whole, but there will also be considerable latitude for classes to vary their routines, usually to suit the teacher's personal style.

*Enforcement of order*

An essential part of the control system is the set of sanctions used for enforcement. The existence of a rule implies the possibility that it will be broken. The fear that the children may refuse to do what the teacher tells them haunts newcomers to teaching, and some teachers never get free of this fear. A whole separate set of norms covers the acts of teacher and pupil when disobedience occurs (see Chapter 10).

Often there will be a well-established procedure for coming to terms with a new teacher. Before his right to be obeyed is conceded, the class will test him out using a carefully graded series of acts of defiance (Fleming, 1944). Thus the pupils discover both what the teacher expects and what he will do if he does not get what he expects. Mercurio (1972) has given

24

a very vivid description of the way in which boys in a traditional New Zealand grammar school brought pressure to bear on new teachers until they were almost always forced against their will to fall in with the traditional use of the cane for selected misdemeanours. It is clear from Mercurio's study that although the teacher appears to hold the power, the pupils in fact may have a decisive influence in the establishment or maintenance of certain norms.

Because the exercise of authority is so often seen by teachers as crucial to their role, the most punishable acts by pupils are those which threaten the teacher's authority. So it is that, although the school may take a dim view of bullying or misappropriation of other people's belongings – acts which are at odds with the moral code of the larger society – it often takes a still more outraged view of insolence or cheek, acts which in many out-of-school settings would not be punishable.

*Transmission of knowledge and skills*

Let us turn now to the instructional function of the teacher, the function which uniquely characterises his role as teacher. The corresponding essential expectation we have for pupils is that they will receive this instruction – that they will learn from their teachers, and that this learning will consist primarily of knowledge and skills, for this is what we usually mean when we speak of instruction.

*Theories and measurements influence expectations*

The study of educational psychology is intended to improve the teacher's giving of instruction and the pupil's receiving of instruction. We can infer something about the instructional aspect of the teacher and pupil roles, therefore, from the preoccupations of educational psychology. These preoccupations can be grouped into two principal areas, the first concerned

25

with such topics as attention, association, remembering, forgetting, and motivation – how learning takes place – and the second concerned with quantitative aspects such as the measurement of initial learning capacity, and the measurement of the results of instruction.

From a study of how learning takes place the teacher is supposed to be able to manipulate the school setting so that conditions are favourable for learning. He is supposed to 'motivate' his pupils, and to present the matter to be learnt in an easily assimilable form adapted to the interests and capacities of his pupils. In all this the pupil's part is by implication a passive one – things are done to or for him – yet paradoxically it is recognised that learning is essentially an activity of the pupil, something done by him.

From a study of the quantitative assessment of capacities and abilities the teacher is supposed to gain two important things: insight into what learning is possible for children of different ages and personalities, and a way of judging his pupils' performance as learners and his own performance as a teacher, by measuring what has been learnt.

As an example of the influence of a knowledge of what is possible on the behaviour teachers expect from pupils, we can refer to current beliefs about reading readiness. If the teacher has been taught that the average child has not the physical or mental equipment to learn to read until he is six years old, the teacher sets his requirements accordingly, and five-year-olds on beginning school are launched on a pre-reading programme. If new discoveries or new techniques revealed that a two-year-old could learn to read (with a feasible investment of man- or woman-power and little or no threat to his psyche), no doubt the teacher would expect pupils to arrive from preschool at age five with a mastery of reading. The teacher's expectations would have an effect not only on his behaviour with his five-year-old pupils, but on parents and preschool teachers, and, through them, on what the children themselves expected. Thus the findings of psychology affect the roles of teacher and pupil; and an important part of the technical equipment of the teacher has to do with the standards he should set for age-groups or individual children in the mastery of instructional material. If he sets standards which are out of reach, he will be dissatisfied with himself as a teacher and the pupil will probably also be made to feel inadequate.

*Evaluating performance*

To facilitate the setting of standards and the assessment of progress, teachers are provided with tools and procedures for measuring achievement, ranging from informal questioning of pupils, and class tests, to standardised tests and external examinations. These procedures are often thought of as indicating the success of the pupil in absorbing instruction, but in fact they also measure the success of the teacher in getting his material across. Tests therefore have a profound effect on the satisfaction both teachers and pupils experience in the performance of their roles. A great deal of anxiety gathers round tests, and complex labelling processes, based on the scores in tests, are used to establish further expectations for performance by pupils. Some very important social consequences arise from this focus of the school on measurement.

First, the satisfactory performance of the teacher's role comes to be demonstrated by the performance of his pupils in tests. Under today's relatively sophisticated conditions, *improvement* in performance counts for more than absolute level of performance amongst many teachers. The pupil who knows all about the subject before his teacher instructs him may afford the teacher no special satisfaction, and the teacher may take pleasure rather in the pupil who *improves* the most. One who does not improve or who loses ground is 'disappointing'; one who improves obtains 'pleasing' results. Report cards reflect the pleasure and displeasure of teachers in the pupils' achievement. Of course, for the teacher to

27

achieve this kind of satisfaction he must be able with some plausibility to take credit for the pupil's improvement. If the improvement were known to coincide with the employment of a private coach by the pupil's parents, the teacher might feel angry rather than pleased at the improvement.

## The ideal pupil

It follows that the 'ideal pupil' from the teacher's point of view is the one who learns a lot, particularly about the matters covered by the tests. He should not always get everything right, however, since this would suggest that he hardly needed teaching. He should be pleased with his success and not blasé about it, and should never suggest that a question or a test is badly worded or worthless. This 'improver' is the pupil who is most rewarding to the teacher, and he is in turn rewarded by the teacher's approval. The common practice of assessing improvement by change in rank order in the class condemns a substantial proportion of the class to deterioration, however well the teacher teaches and the pupils learn. The pupil who, through relative lack of ability or motivation or for any other reason, fails to absorb the instruction offered, is not performing his role as a pupil in the way the teacher and the school would like, and so reaps disapproval and is discouraged in his performance. If any alternative role presents itself as a source of satisfaction, this pupil is only too ready to abandon the attempt to learn : he might, for instance, concentrate on getting a laugh from his fellow-pupils instead of getting approval from the teacher.

An alternative to objective achievement in school subjects as a source of teacher approval is a reputation for 'trying'. The pupil who successfully performs the role of trier but fails to achieve may get sympathy and extra help instead of disapproval for failing. The trier looks attentive, submits to the teacher's authority in matters of control, writes something in his book even if it is full of mistakes, and looks suitably chagrined when his errors are pointed out to him. This kind of behaviour has better survival value in the classroom than the opposite kind and is perhaps more easily learnt by middle-class than working-class children.

But in general the concern of teachers for cognitive achievement of a kind that can be measured leads to the rejection by the school of pupils who do not achieve. They are rejected in many ways: by being given worse teachers, left aside as hopeless, ridiculed, castigated, punished. In relation to a norm which prescribes achievement, they are deviant.

A second important social consequence of the school's achievement norms is the elevation of knowledge and skills which can be readily measured at the expense of those which cannot. In theory the aim of a school may be 'to extend all pupils to the utmost of their ability, to develop habits of industry, obedience, self-reliance and send out into the world young men and women of character', a statement typical of school prospectuses. But in practice these outcomes are so hard to measure that teachers, naturally enough, often settle for aims such as getting the maximum number of pupils to pass their O-levels or A-levels. The process of adapting school procedures to the exigencies of measurement techniques is taken one stage further when teaching success is judged by the ratio of examination passes to pupils entering for the examination. This may lead teachers to discourage some pupils from entering, and amongst those discouraged there are likely to be a few who, with luck on their side, would have passed.

*Evaluation and the pupil's career*

Current trends in internal assessment have an important bearing on the teacher-pupil relationship. As long as the agencies of instruction remain separate from those of evaluation, that is as long as there are external examinations, the pupil and teacher are on the same side. The teacher does what he can to ensure that as many as possible of his pupils pass. But when the teacher becomes the judge of the results of his teaching, he is usually constrained in one way or another to see that some of his pupils fail, in order to convince everyone that his standards are high enough. And in deciding who are to be the failures the teacher almost inevitably takes into account the learning history of his pupils, allowing part of the credit for qualities other than present competence. Such considerations led Illich (1971) to assert:

> To detach competence from curriculum, enquiries into a man's learning history must be made taboo, like enquiries into his political affiliation, church attendance, lineage, sex habits, or racial background.

Whatever useful features there are in internal assessment, combining the roles of instructor and assessor in the person of the teacher is likely to have adverse effects on the teacher-pupil relationship, to lead to distrust and deceit on the part of the pupils. External examinations, in spite of the tensions they induce, do serve to diminish the dependence of the pupils on making the right impression on their teachers. Standardised tests and programmed material and various self-testing devices similarly avoid to a considerable extent dependence of pupils on teachers for assessment of their worthiness. When the teacher points out mistakes and assigns low grades, pupils almost inevitably interpret this as implying disapproval. The pupils who wrote *Letter to a Teacher* (Barbiana, 1970) felt very strongly that a teacher who gave them a failing mark was rejecting them:

> A helping hand from you could make the difference. You did stretch out a hand – but to topple him once and for all.... If only you were able to say, 'Why don't you come back to school? I've passed you, just so that you can come back. Without you, school somehow has lost its flavour.'

There is a further subtle menace in exposing pupils to the judgment of teachers. The teacher is in a powerful position to make his own expectations come true. Once he has formed a judgment, on whatever evidence, he tends to act on it, urging pupils he has decided are good to do better work and accepting poorer work from those he has judged less able. Henceforth when he marks their work he is more likely to give the pupil he calls 'good' a high mark, and the 'poor' pupil a low mark. The 'good' pupil's lapses from good behaviour may pass without comment, while the 'bad' pupil's lapses are underlined – 'Just what I would expect from you, Saunders'.

The teacher probably also communicates his expectations to other teachers, and the other teachers as well as the pupil himself adjust their expectations accordingly. The school is thus an ideal setting for the operation of the self-fulfilling prophecy, and this is a very serious risk to which pupils are exposed in performing their role.

*Conclusion*

The role of the pupil as the one who is instructed is thus a complex one, involving learning the right things at the right rate and with the right display of enthusiasm, and coming to terms with his own shortcomings as they are variously revealed to him by assessment devices and teacher judgments. All pupils will fail at times to learn what is set for them, and some pupils will fail almost all the time. To survive in the classroom they must find a way of interpreting their occasional or regular failures so that they retain their self-respect and the respect of others who matter to them. Their classmates are very important in this search, as we shall see in Chapter 8.

# 4

## Candidates for salvation

> This is my son, mine own Telemachus,
> To whom I leave the sceptre and the isle –
> Well-loved of me, discerning to fulfil
> This labour, by slow prudence to make mild
> A rugged people, and thro' soft degrees
> Subdue them to the useful and the good.

The task which Tennyson's Ulysses allots to his son in this passage is closely akin to one of the main tasks teachers are expected to perform for pupils. The pupil, a young savage, is by the 'discernment and slow prudence' of the teacher to be 'subdued to the useful and the good'. The teacher is, in less colourful terms, the missionary or reformer assigned to continue the task of socialisation begun by the parents. The beginnings of the parents' missionary activities have been vividly described by Fraiberg (1959) who says that the second year of a child's life is the time when the missionaries arrive 'bearing culture to the joyful savage' by teaching him to drink from a cup, use a potty, and avoid messy objects.

### Reforming zeal

The missionary motive as it influences the outlook of teachers has been documented in one section of an interesting investigation into teachers' attitudes by Jackson (1968). He discusses the satisfactions reported by some outstanding primary school teachers from their work. It is clear from his evidence that the enthusiasm of many of these teachers is closely bound up with a missionary spirit. One teacher remarked:

> I think it's like missionary work. I've always been very socially-minded, and I think that we really do have a lot of work to do right in these communities, not just in the under-privileged ones.

Even in the prosaic pages of *Half Our Future* (Newsom Report, 1963) we read that the practical subjects 'offer creative and *civilising* experiences beneficial to *all pupils*' (my italics). In a general way, salvation, if not from the fires of hell, at least from the disastrous consequences of cultural deprivation, has long been part of the goal of schools. It was so for the Sunday Schools which marked the beginnings of a move towards universal primary education in eighteenth century England, and for the kindergarten movement in its early stages, and for Headstart programmes in the United States, and for the movement towards comprehensive schools in Britain, to name a few instances. Carter (1966) refers to public education in Britain as a 'rescue operation'.

A similar missionary zeal often infuses the work of educators dealing with children out of school. Hogan (1970), a scout master, writes of one of his scouts:

> No attempt to persuade him to take any of our training at all seriously met with the slightest success. This, of course, was an insupportable affront to the dedicated educator. I set myself to bring about his conversion.

Hogan was furious when the boy, acting in his usual unregenerate way, produced a slipshod model plane, and 'even more furious when the wretched thing clawed and crabbed its way through the air to take the specified distance'. But he was proud and happy when the boy's attitude eventually improved.

33

So strong is the missionary impulse of some teachers that they may go out of their way to acquire in their class troubled, 'lost' children unwanted by other teachers, in the hope of succeeding where others have failed (Jackson, 1968). There is even a sense of urgency, that if some of the children do not get the help they need now, it may be too late.

## Candidates for reform

The missionary role of the teacher carries some interesting implications for the role of the pupil. Apparently it will not matter if the pupil is at first a veritable savage. It may even be an advantage from the teacher's point of view, provided the savage is amenable to reform. One cannot perform the role of rescuer with a pupil who has already been rescued.

Reform should not be too slow, or it will not be visible to the teacher, although some teachers have a remarkable capacity for delayed satisfaction. Grace (1972) quotes a 63-year-old male grammar school teacher as saying:

> In later years we find many of the less able boys blossomed out into excellent leaders of society, with a clear sense of gratitude for the teaching they received at school.

Reform will presumably be shown by the pupil's abandoning his former uncivilised ways, whether of ungrammatical speech, bad manners, lack of breeding, untidy dress, lack of self-control, maladjustment, naughtiness or laziness, and acquiring the virtues advocated by the missionary. It is assumed that the missionary is superior to the pupil in recognising virtue and pointing the way. The missionary is expected to be himself a model of virtue and the pupil is expected to copy this model. The teacher is to supply a better model than the typical adult.

Improvement in the child should come about in such a way that the teacher feels able to take some credit. It should

34

happen when the teacher has charge of the pupil and not after the pupil has passed on to his next teacher. The good behaviour should be most obvious in the presence of the teacher, not in his absence. It will be hard for the teacher to take credit for an improvement in, say, a child's behaviour at home, if there has been no improvement at school. In short, the improvement should be such as can plausibly be attributed to the teacher's intervention. 'When you've had a child who had been a severe problem and some way you've reached him and done something for him, that's a real thrill' (Jackson, 1968). In his more reasonable moments the teacher may know that improvement might have taken place without his intervention, but 'Even if it was just their development you give yourself credit'.

The view of a pupil as an uncivilised creature in need of reform is a view teachers often hold, but it is not a view pupils themselves are likely to share. And even if the pupils saw themselves as needing the teacher's help to change their ways, they could easily resent their reformer. Gratitude is a difficult emotion for a mature person to feel and an improbable one for the child who is being 'subdued to the useful and the good'. So teachers are likely only rarely to receive gratitude from pupils for their missionary efforts. If from time to time a pupil performs with distinction the role of 'savage-becoming-civilised', and shows appreciation of the teacher's efforts, this occasional reward may sustain the teacher's enthusiasm. Excessive gratitude might seem presumptuous in a pupil, but in later life the former pupil, looking back on his schooldays, may appropriately recognise and refer to the great debt he owes to his teachers.

The reforming task of the teacher receives more emphasis in the primary school than in the secondary school. Amongst secondary schools, the secondary modern school pays more attention to this task than the grammar school (for instance, see Musgrove and Taylor, 1969). But even the academic subject-centred teachers of senior grammar school pupils like to think of themselves as helpful to pupils with problems, so a sprinkling of pupils with suitable problems requiring help may be very acceptable to these teachers too.

'Savage-becoming-civilised' is, then, an important component of the pupil role from the standpoint of many teachers. It provides a slot into which reformable pupils can comfortably fit. But it is not, we surmise, a natural role to the child. He learns it in response to the teacher's missionary expectations. It is possible for him not only to learn to change his ways, but also to learn first to have ways that need changing. Might the teacher at times help to create in the child the condition he hopes to remedy? This can happen in very subtle ways, as when a teacher with a new class warns pupils against behaviour that had not entered their heads, thereby indicating an expectation that such behaviour will sometimes occur.

## The pupil looks ahead

A special kind of shaping of pupils' attitudes and behaviour is that known as 'anticipatory socialisation'. This aims to produce behaviour which is not so much admirable in the pupil's present as advantageous for his future. The well-known public schools consciously form their pupils into a leadership mould in anticipation of their future status. In like manner medical students presenting themselves for oral examinations may be expected to dress and deport themselves in a manner befitting not their present student role but their future doctor role. The hair-length controversy reported by Hargreaves (1967) was seen by the teachers as important because of the pupils' future occupational roles. The underlying assumption is made that present behaviour of the pupil will continue in some future role and this present behaviour should therefore be appropriate to the future role rather than to the present. On close examination a great deal of the behaviour urged on pupils has this forward-looking quality. Yet it may be much harder to practise parts of a future role in advance than it is to assume the complete role when the time comes. It would be useful to have the behaviour in one's repertoire, but it is tiresome to be called on to use it outside the role for which it is designed. Requiring the medical student to be well turned out for his oral examination is a way of checking whether he has in his repertoire the behaviour thought appropriate to the profession. He need not be expected to exercise this behaviour throughout his student activities, but in practice he may well find that he is expected to dress more conservatively and behave more decorously at lectures than arts students, in anticipation of his membership of a conservative and dignified profession.

*Conclusion*

Our consideration of the missionary element in the role of the teacher, then, leads us to recognise that the pleasure of the teacher in his teaching is enhanced by having pupils who need reform and respond to the teacher's efforts to reform them, pupils who are initially somewhat uncouth, thoughtless, mischievous or otherwise reprehensible and who are willing to be redeemed and to model themselves on the ideal offered to them. These pupils are performing their role in a way which, because it is satisfying to the teacher, improves the quality of interaction between teacher and pupil and confirms each in his role relationship. At a sophisticated level, pupils develop a concept of themselves as they hope to be in adult life, and may look to their teachers for indications of the behaviour to adopt in order to qualify for future membership of their chosen group.

The role of savage-becoming-civilised accords well with the child role in society, as seen by many adults, but it requires a future orientation and a humility about present competence that are alien to many pupils. For these pupils there may be conflict between their role as they see it and their role as seen through the eyes of their teachers.

37

# 5

## Natural enemies

In *Tom Brown's Schooldays* (Hughes, 1948) we read:

> ... for years afterwards ... the masters' hands were against him, and his against them. And he regarded them, as a matter of course, as his natural enemies.

At one time or another every pupil looks on his teacher more or less as an enemy. He fears him, is frustrated by him or angry with him, enjoys seeing him embarrassed, and tries to deceive him or score over him.

As long ago as 1932 Waller drew attention to the essential opposition between the standpoints of teacher and pupil:

> Teacher and pupil confront each other in the school with an original conflict of desires ... with attitudes from which the underlying hostility can never be altogether removed.

This, Waller points out, comes from the fact that whereas the teacher must impose on pupils the tasks laid down by the adult world, and must establish and maintain a social order devoted to accomplishing those tasks, the pupil on the other hand spontaneously seeks to express himself in ways which are opposed to the teacher's wishes; so that 'in so far as the aims of either are realized, it is at the sacrifice of the aims of the other'.

38

## Pupils hide their shortcomings

Even when teacher and pupil are mature adults, conflict between their interests and goals is generally inherent in their relationship. At the university level the influence of the lecturer on the evaluation of the student's merit, and hence on his career prospects, undermines the friendly relationship that both may desire. The relationship between students and lecturers is revealed as one involving a measure of mistrust and deceit by a number of ploys in which students engage. The student disguises his ignorance by leading discussion away from points on which he is unsure, or by invoking illness to excuse failure to complete work assigned or poor performance. He emphasises his knowledge and interest by consulting the lecturer after the lecture on points meant to show how serious and committed he is. He disagrees about relatively unimportant details to show his independence of thought. In short, he deliberately manages his encounters with his lecturer so as to present himself in the most favourable light.

School pupils feel a similar need of vigilance lest the teacher gain possession of damaging information about them. Lacey (1970) suggests that the teacher, on account of his role in selecting and grading pupils, is more rigorously excluded from some aspects of student sub-culture than other adults. Pupils completing questionnaires for a non-teacher commonly said 'You won't show these answers to any of the teachers, will you?'

## Pupils defy their teachers

Amongst school pupils, to score over a teacher is an admired form of behaviour. Even the well-documented expectation that pupils have of their teachers, that the teachers will control them and teach them, cannot be taken as evidence that the pupils intend to go along with the teachers' attempts to do this. An eighteen-year-old university student expressed a

39

typical pupil attitude when, on being reprimanded by a warden for a breach of the rules of his hall of residence, he said, 'It's your job to make the rules and our job to break them'. We would regard this as a childish attitude, but it points us to an important component of the role of the pupil.

*Resentment of authority*

This kind of antagonism is an aspect of the relationship between pupil and teacher not often discussed by teachers. The teacher prefers to see himself as the pupil's friend and benefactor, whether or not the pupil recognises it. Yet antagonism is to some extent implicit in all relationships between superiors and inferiors, between those who confer benefits and those who receive them. It exists in the even more important parent-child relationship. The parent, representing the establishment, necessarily thwarts some of the child's desires and at times invokes the child's resentment or hatred. Since the parent-child relationship is likely to provide the child with a pattern for later relationships with those in authority, opposition to teachers on the part of pupils has some of its roots in the frustrations suffered by the child at the hands of his parents.

Resentment towards parents is difficult and dangerous to express. Basic and permanent emotional ties are threatened. Even becoming aware of hatred towards parents often gives rise to strong guilt feelings in children.

Pupils can feel guilty towards teachers too, although the feeling is likely to be less crippling. Fleming (1961) describes a hostile relationship with a teacher that gave rise to feelings of guilt in the pupils. Fleming and his classmates persecuted mercilessly a master who was at first cocksure, with a grating personality, but who became jumpy, irritable and maladjusted and finally died in a mild influenza epidemic, leaving the pupils with the guilty feeling that they had somehow 'hounded him into his grave'.

40

Notwithstanding this example, it is generally easier and safer for children to express hostility to a teacher than to a parent, especially if the hostility can find an institutional outlet through time-honoured rituals in which many pupils share. We shall shortly examine a number of these rituals.

First, however, it should be pointed out that children are unlikely to be aware of the sources of their hostile feelings, or to understand their own behaviour which derives from those feelings. Hostile attitudes may find safe expression in common rituals, or they may appear as open defiance (challenging the teacher's role as disciplinarian) or as refusal or inability to learn (challenging his role as instructor). A boy who had previously made good progress and enjoyed school suddenly ceased to learn and resisted going to school. He could not explain what was wrong, but the reason became apparent when his mother visited the school. She found that his new teacher bore a marked physical resemblance to the boy's father who had left home several years before after a number of violent episodes.

Teachers, as well as evoking undeserved hostility from pupils on account of the pupils' family experiences, may of course bring to their relationships with pupils their own resentments, derived from childhood conflict with parents, brothers or sisters, and from adult conflict with husband or wife or children. Morris (1967) points out that 'every teacher drags into the classroom the residues of his own childhood'. Thus pupils and teachers alike, in acting out their roles, are influenced by their out-of-school relationships both past and present.

Most of the time the hostility component of the teacher-pupil relationship is kept within bounds, and its institutionalisation in the form of a number of rituals helps to keep it under control. The same rituals perhaps also intensify and perpetuate the feelings of hostility, since the pupil learns through the rituals what feelings to have and when to have them.

41

*Ritual expression of hostility*

Chants popular with generations of pupils, often over a long time and a wide area, epitomise their antagonism towards their teachers. The Opies (1959) give a number of examples of chants which attack or ridicule teachers:

> Mr. MacDonald is a good man,
>> He goes to church on Sunday,
>> He prays to God to give him strength,
>> To whip the boys on Monday.
>
>> Sir is kind and sir is gentle,
>> Sir is strong and sir is mental.
>
>> Teacher, teacher, I don't like you,
>> If you don't mark my sums right
>> – I shall spike you.

(pricking a drawing of the teacher with pins.)

...

Another chant which does not appear in the Opies' collection is:

> 12 and 12 are 24,
> Kick the teacher out the door.

Some, like the following, express dislike of school rather than teachers:

>> Two more days and we will be
>> Out of the gates of misery.
>> No more spelling, no more sums,
>> No more whacks upon our bums.

This last, which has very many variations often more colourful than the above on account of the swear words used, sets forth a fundamental norm of the pupil culture, that school

42

is miserable. Yet probably the majority of children in most schools enjoy school and find the school holidays tedious. Even low stream pupils in the study by Hargreaves (1967) usually found more to interest them at school than away: 'It's not really worth staying off. It's boring. That's when I come back, when I'm bored.'

Adults of course foster the view of school as tedious or unpleasant by linking school with work and contrasting it with play and holidays. The pupils who wrote *Letter to a Teacher* (Barbiana, 1970) point out that time off school is used by adults as a reward or treat, thus conveying that the pupils are expected to dislike school.

Chants, then, offer pupils an institutionalised expression of dislike for teachers and schools. Another form in which antagonism between pupils and teachers finds expression is using nicknames. This custom is almost universal. Teachers are usually somewhat uncomfortable about it and pretend not to hear when a pupil inadvertently refers to Old Ma Brown or Grumpy Mac or Fishy Rowe in their presence.

Young children adopt a special method of dealing with their feelings towards teachers when they 'play school'. The game of teachers and pupils has a perennial popularity and a stereotyped form. The teacher is harsh, bossy and arbitrary and the pupils cheeky and disobedient. The Opies (1969) give some examples, from which the following is taken:

'The most favourite game played in school is "Schools",' says an Edinburgh 9-year-old. 'Tommy is the headmaster, Robin is the school-teacher, and I am the naughty boy. Robin asks us what are two and two. We say they are six. He gives us the belt. Sometimes we run away from school and what a commotion! Tommy and Robin run after us. When we are caught we are taken back and everybody is sorry.'

Clearly playing 'Schools' is a way to turn the table on real school: a child can become a teacher, pupils can

43

be naughty, and fun can be made of punishments. It is noticeable, too, that the most demure child in the real classroom is liable to become the most talkative when the canes are make-believe.

The acting out of these roles has a strong appeal even for pupils who have never experienced teachers who fit the stereotype, and it is hard to avoid the conclusion that the games serve a useful purpose in the children's lives. They may sharpen the pupils' conception of their roles by exaggerating in cartoon fashion some aspects of the roles; and they may increase the feeling of solidarity among pupils and assert independence of adult pressures. Amongst older pupils, 'taking off' a teacher may serve similar purposes. At any rate the games clearly show teachers and pupils cast as opponents, and this is obviously fun.


*Backstage behaviour*

Chants, nicknames, and games of school are reserved for pupils' backstage occasions. On official occasions, in classroom or assembly hall, pupils conform more or less to the official norms, but schools also provide a great deal of scope for unofficial activity, from unsupervised parts of the playground during breaks to moments in the classroom when the teacher's back is turned. As pupils move between the different settings a school provides, their behaviour can thus oscillate between respect and friendliness on the one hand and disrespect and hostility on the other, just as the teacher's behaviour changes when he closes the staff-room door. The oscillation is a sign not of inconsistency in the pupil's or teacher's personality but of intelligent mastery of the subtle changes in role expectations between one situation and another. As long as the situations can be kept from overlapping no difficulties need arise.

Overlapping is prevented in part by allocation of separate

territories to teachers and pupils for some of the time. Teachers in their staffroom are safe from pupils, and there are playground areas where pupils are relatively safe from teachers. The problem of maintaining some separateness is more serious at boarding schools than at day schools, but it seems often to be solved rather well. In *Tom Brown's School-days* we recognise two separate worlds of pupils and teachers. Indeed the worlds are so distinct that stories about boarding school life in schoolboys' and schoolgirls' papers can be written so that the teachers hardly feature as personalities. The delegation of some of the teachers' authority to senior pupils who are made prefects frees the teachers from other-wise unavoidable contacts with pupils and allows the pupils to socialise one another in accordance with norms embedded in the tradition of the school.

Pupils expect teachers to refrain from an assortment of behaviours which could be called spying. Teachers should not appear suddenly and unexpectedly in the pupils' midst. They should manage to give warning of their approach. They should not be in places where they might overhear pupils without the pupils knowing. They should not ask questions or set exercises which might make the pupil disclose damaging in-formation about himself or another pupil. They should not frequent the out-of-school haunts of pupils.

*Pupils with something to hide*

Goffman (1969) describes what he calls 'expression games', which are techniques a person uses to control or manage the impression he makes on other people. Characteristics of such games as described by Goffman are to be found in pupil-teacher interaction. The teacher at first sight seems to have much better opportunities than his pupils to conceal his own attitudes, motives and behaviour. But in some respects the advantage is with the pupils, for there are dozens or hun-dreds of pupils any one of whom may catch the teacher off

45

guard in school or outside it. Moreover, the damage to the teacher's reputation if he is caught out is more serious by virtue of his position, which requires him to behave in a consistently exemplary fashion.

Pupils have initially the disadvantage of inexperience in trying to conceal things from teachers, and they are threatened by the teacher's ready access to their means of concealment of material objects and guilty knowledge. The teacher can order the pupil to expose the contents of his desk, pocket or mouth, or require him to divulge information.

But pupils quickly gain experience and play expression games with great ingenuity and subtlety, so that a great deal of the pupils' lives is effectively sealed off from access by the teacher. Sometimes teachers gain access to information about pupils by getting them to write diaries or essays or take part in discussions in which the pupils are likely to let slip information about normally reserved areas of their lives. However, pupils often resent this, and even the most naïve pupils exercise some control over the information they communicate. Pupils can do this because they can to some extent put themselves in the place of the teacher and judge how likely it is that the teacher would disapprove.

Goffman's description of the manoeuvres of people to extricate themselves when caught in acts of concealment rings a bell in the experience of teachers. If feigning innocence fails, a pupil may claim ignorance of the rule, attempt a redefinition of the situation, or assume an air of penitence. A girl may burst into tears, a manoeuvre which makes a male teacher feel a brute. Aspects of behaviour when caught out are further discussed in Chapter 11.

The skill of the pupil at expression games may have an important effect on his career, influencing his class placement, the teacher's willingness to interact with him (and hence to teach him), his examination results, the comments on his report ('tries hard' instead of 'work deteriorating') and the testimonial he gets when he leaves school. The unskilful pupil, clumsy at concealing his acts and inept when he is caught out, repeatedly comes into conflict with his teachers.

However, most hated by teachers is the ultra slick pupil whose performance is so good that the teacher 'sees through' him and dubs him 'insincere'.

Perhaps girls in general surpass boys in impression management skills and so seem less often to come into conflict with their teachers.

## Constructive aspects of conflict

We need not regard conflict between pupils and teachers as wholly bad. Conflict fosters solidarity amongst pupils. Solidarity is one of the prime needs of children confronted by an alien world. It is a need that the modern small family cannot meet, especially in the close confines of a middle-class home. In a large family the children may escape at times from the society of adults and live in a world of their own. Neighbourhood peer groups in working-class areas may meet the same needs for escape from adult oversight. But children in middle-class families do not have many opportunities to test their attitudes and beliefs, their skills and knowledge, amongst their peers in places where they are not supervised or overheard by adults. The opportunities they get at school are for them doubly important. In opposing adult values and demands they close their ranks and gain support from one another.

As a target for this opposition a teacher is, as we have seen, in many ways more useful than a parent, since he can be attacked or hated with less disturbance to the child's self.

To indulge in expressions of hostility to teachers, pupils thus need a place where teachers will not intrude. They need such a place even more than teachers, for a teacher is permitted to say insulting things to a pupil but a pupil is not normally permitted to insult a teacher. But the teachers' need for privacy is usually conceded while the pupils' need is usually ignored.

Another important function of conflict is to provide excitement or relieve boredom. There is a risk in defying a teacher openly or covertly. In the game of having the teacher on, 'bad' pupils defy the teacher while 'good' pupils enjoy the fun. To make a teacher mad relieves the monotony as nothing else does. The pupils who are prepared to expose themselves to the teacher's wrath may thus achieve great status amongst their peers, and may be happy even to submit to caning in return for status.

This does not of course mean that open warfare between teacher and pupils should be fostered to enliven the day, but simply that teachers need not feel they have failed whenever pupils are antagonistic. Nor need the teacher try to remain quite unruffled. Some teachers recognise the appropriateness of a display of anger when provoked. Blishen (1966) describes a fictional but by no means fantastic teacher:

> He was capable of the most tremendous pretences of rage. When a boy was behaving badly Charles would stop everything and stand stock still, a kind of Jove-like amazement and fury creeping over his whole body till he was stiff and, as it were, resonant with doom. He drew to himself in this way, the attention of everyone in the class. They watched him fascinated ... Then followed a process difficult to describe because it was, and was meant to be, difficult to focus. Charles became a flurry, a whirlwind of indefinable castigatory gestures, hovering over his victim, not touching him but giving him an awful sense of being buffeted as though by some furious eagle. Then he would groan. 'I am ... speechless,' he would say.

This account makes very clear the dramatic quality of much of the interaction between teacher and pupil. In the example, the teacher has a highly idiosyncratic version of the angry-teacher role, but the pupils have not the slightest difficulty in recognising the role and responding with the appropriate cowed-pupil behaviour. All boredom has been banished. At the same time the interaction fits into expected patterns of maintenance of status of pupil and teacher, and social order is preserved.

Perhaps the transformation of the situation into a dramatic performance is the most successful way of defusing hostility. By establishing a dramatic ritual for use when order is threatened, a teacher may be able to recast the pupils in the role of interested audience instead of hostile opponents.

*Summary*

We have seen that conflict between pupils and teachers must be accepted as inevitable and even to some extent useful. Some of the consequences of conflict for the interaction between pupils and teachers and for their separate worlds have been considered. Later chapters about the pupil peer group, the rule-breakers and the miscreant role deal further with some aspects of the antagonism between pupils and teachers.

# 6

## Customers and clients

The complexity of the role of the pupil is evident from the very diverse components which make up the role. We have seen that pupils are cast at times in the role of antagonists to their teachers, and at times in the role of potential converts. A third component which differs radically from both of these others is the role of the customer choosing or rejecting the benefits offered by the school. The benefits take many forms: knowledge, skills, experience; years of school attendance seen as an asset in the search for a job; assorted certificates, diplomas and testimonials; membership of sports and other teams; the prestige of attendance at 'good' schools; and, not least, fun, which may be a principal benefit for a section of the pupils, as Hargreaves (1967) has shown very clearly.

Somewhat akin to the role of pupil as customer is the client role in which advice or help is sought. These aspects of the pupil role we shall now explore.

Especially when pupils are young, the role of customer is performed for them largely by their parents. It is true that the customer role is harder to discern when schooling is compulsory and there is no choice of schools. However, choices are exercised by parents before and after the age of compulsory schooling, although even outside this age range the choice is often more apparent than real. The pupil whose school achievement is poor, or whose parents are short of

50

money or uninterested in education, or whose friends all leave school, has little real choice.

## Ways of making choices

But even during the years of compulsory schooling, choices are made in a number of interesting ways.

First, the pupil who does not like school may stay away. Hargreaves (1967) found that low stream boys were absent more often than boys in high streams, and postulated that this reflected the failure of the school to offer them anything they wanted. Parents, too, if they do not value what the school offers, may keep children (especially girls) at home to help in family crises or for minor illnesses, when other parents who value education see that their children attend.

Second, pupils who are disenchanted with school may come to school but refuse to learn, by not attending to their work or by disregarding the demands of their teachers. Teachers of these pupils usually moderate their demands, so the customer's wishes do influence the school's wares. The pupils may even succeed in turning class periods into an entertainment. Lack of commitment to the learning goals of the school may characterise sections of school classes or whole classes, constituting part of an anti-academic subculture. Even pupils who are for the most part committed to learning are at times unresponsive, causing teachers to modify their teaching.

Third, even within the system there is scope for choice, and pupils or their parents make choices amongst courses, subjects, projects and optional extra activities. Often, however, parents and pupils are ill-informed about their rights to choose or about the choices available and the consequences of one choice or another, and so they fail to exercise a choice or they exercise it poorly. The school may discourage the exercise of choices by parents and pupils on the grounds that they are ill-informed and apt to make wrong choices, and this discouragement may take the form of supplying too little information about the scope for choosing and the consequences, or notifying parents only when the choice has been made and it seems too late to object, or using guidance or counselling to channel pupils in the direction chosen for them by the school.

A fourth method of exercising rights as a customer or consumer is by complaining, criticising or protesting. Bernbaum (1971), commenting on Countesthorpe College a few months after its setting up, noted:

> Many parents have already expressed their anxieties that the school might not meet their expectations with respect to both instruction in subjects and social advancement.

Parents who are dissatisfied with the education supplied by the school may harass the school, or the authority or board responsible for the school; they may write letters to local papers; or they may encourage their children to oppose the teachers. Dissatisfied pupils can wage their private battles against the establishment, or band together to express disagreement, and demand some part in the making of the decisions which affect them. Both parents and pupils may find a press which is ready to publicise their cause when they have complaints to make.

Lacey (1970) recorded a number of cases of 'articulate, ambitious, middle-class parents who were able to manipulate the ideology of the school' on behalf of their child. For instance, parents who knew one of the teachers convinced him that their child had the background and potentiality to be placed in a higher stream than his test results warranted, and would be adversely affected if not so placed; and that the child's present failure to achieve at a higher level was merely the result of a 'temporary psychological difficulty'. The teachers responded to this kind of pleading because the child came from a 'cultured' family. This kind of manipulation is closely parallel to the activities of the customer who by knowing the right person and giving the right reasons

52

wangles a seat in the aeroplane when others are told the plane is full. One of the many advantages the middle-class child has over the working-class child in getting educated is the ability of his parents to drive a better bargain on his behalf. Schools may even avoid unfavourable placement of children whose parents might make a fuss, just as the butcher may avoid giving his inferior meat to the housewife whose potential for complaint is known.

## Buying education

The best of all ways of exercising choice is open only to those parents who can afford to opt out of the state school system and send their children to fee-charging schools. These schools must offer what is wanted by their customers if they are to stay in business. We need only read the prospectuses of these schools to see how they present their wares to appeal to prospective customers. A typical advertisement for a girls' secondary school mentioned Christian values, small classes, careful supervision, sound study habits, examination successes, sporting honours, cultural activities, speech training, high grade accommodation and moderate fees, ending with this statement:

> Truth ... Honour ... Virtue ... these are the basic qualities in life for girls.... College aims to develop these qualities.
> Your daughter's education is the most important investment you can make – in years to come she will value and appreciate your foresight in sending her to ... College.

The less adequately the state schools meet the demands of the consumers of education, the better is the market for the fee-charging schools. Conversely, it is being proposed that the fee-charging schools should be abolished partly so that their present customers may exert pressure to improve the state schools.

Some families unable to afford fees may still be able to

53

arrange to shift from one educational district to another, thus choosing within the state system. Once again it is the middle-class parents who can manoeuvre in this way to get a better deal for their children.

### Choosing at preschool and university levels

At the preschool level an interesting state of affairs exists. Education at this level is in very short supply. It is available on the one hand to parents who can pay fees, and on the other hand to children stigmatised as deprived or at risk. To qualify for free preschool education for her children a mother may find it helps to have several preschool children, be a solo parent, live in a poor house or at least in a poor area, go out to work or have trouble coping. 'Choosing' preschool education may be a matter of getting into one or more of these categories.

At the university level parents may still be directly involved in their children's choice to continue with their education. They exert more influence at the middle-class level than the lower class level, for if the parents are judged able to contribute, their children are not given adequate bursaries to be independent of parental support. The parents can thus give or withhold their support even when their 'children' are in their twenties.

In all these ways parents and pupils behave as customers trying to choose the kind and amount of education they want. Nevertheless the limits of choice are narrow for most parents and pupils. At best they have to accept a package deal. They cannot shop for English at one school and physics at another.

### The teachers' claim to know best

Musgrove and Taylor (1969) devote a chapter to a discussion of the assumption by teachers in the last 100 years of most of the decision-making in British schools. They claim that the

54

rights of the parents have been progressively eroded partly in consequence of the efforts which have been made to enhance the status of the teaching profession. The more the teacher becomes the expert who alone knows what is best for the pupil, the less say can be allowed to the parent. It has become more and more apparent that parent-teacher groups are regarded by the school as a means of indoctrinating parents, of persuading them to accept what the teachers have decided is best, rather than as a forum where teachers and parents can share the unique insights each has gained. The burgeoning guidance and counselling movement, although in theory designed to help pupils to formulate and achieve their own personal goals, seems likewise in practice to be another powerful instrument in the hands of the school to get pupils to follow the line the school has chosen. In North America where it is held that teachers have never been able to go as far with their claim to know best, counselling services are used extensively to get pupils to accept the decisions teachers have made in the pupils' interest.

In so far as pupils or their parents have a right to the customer role, the teachers' claim to know best has to be moderated. This is one of the basic issues taken up by Illich (1971) in *Deschooling Society*. He proposes that people should learn only what they want to learn, from teachers of their own choice. To achieve this, he advocates finding some alternative way of slotting people into jobs. Paper qualifications would be abolished, and fitness for jobs assessed on the basis of performance in job-related tasks.

### Being 'hooked' on school

Illich claims that the mass of the 'customers' of the education system, who have not had access to as much education as they wanted, have been indoctrinated so that they believe their lack of school attendance stamps them as inferior. Consequently they believe that their children would cease to be

55

inferior if they attended school for a longer time. These people are 'hooked' on school. They have been sold on the value of a product (time spent in school) which is really worthless, and, like consumers who have been misled by false advertising, they need to be rescued from their erroneous and expensive belief. They are threatened by the monopoly schools have on the provision of qualifications. 'Instead of equalising chances, the school system has monopolised their distribution.'

Illich's proposals would doubtless work well for the transmission of some kinds of skills. In fact this is more or less the way we learn to drive a car. We learn when we are ready to learn, from the teacher of our choice. But the very fact to which Illich calls attention, the gullibility of the consumer of education, would rapidly lead to a dangerous chaos if purveyors of education were left to compete for customers in a field from which established systems had been eliminated. Time spent on courses and progress through a recognised curriculum may be an inadequate indication of competence to practise as a doctor or an engineer, but a method of assessing fitness to practise that leaves these factors out of account would have to rely on even more dubious evidence.

### 'Free play' and pupil choice

Most of our discussion of choices up to this point has centred round choices amongst schools and amongst courses or subjects. It is interesting to look at developments in choice of activities within a school or course as another aspect of the customer role in education. Preschool programmes have been specially active in offering meaningful choices to pupils for several decades. 'Free play' conditions provide a variety of alternative activities from which the child is free to select what appeals to him for the time being. It is assumed that the child himself is the best judge of what he should do, just as he is usually the best judge of the amount of food he needs. The

56

teacher's role is to help him decide and then to help him accomplish what he wants to do, a role very similar to the role which a good architect or landscape gardener performs in relation to his client. But the teacher also sets the stage, and in so doing restricts the choice of the child to activities valued by the teacher, just as the buyer for the department store determines what goods will be available to be chosen by the customer.

Implicit in allowing the child to choose is a belief that what he *wants* and what he *needs* will, under the restricted conditions of choice provided, be nearly enough in harmony, so that his development will not be impeded by his choices. This might at first seem improbable: how could so immature a person know what is good for him? But a young child cannot at all easily be induced to do what he does not want to do anyway, however much we are convinced it is what he 'needs' to do. So in practice it is reasonable to rely on the stage-setting activity of the teacher to limit the child's choice to selected beneficial alternatives known to appeal to preschool children. (In this god-like activity the teacher is greatly aided by fashions. The brightly-coloured, hygienically-enamelled blocks of one decade give place to the unadorned natural wooden blocks of the next decade.)

In spite of the limitations imposed by the teacher, the very young child thus exercises the role of customer more effectively than he will when he becomes a primary school pupil. If he does not like the feel or the colour of the clay he can choose to paint, and if the blocks are in a gloomy corner he can look at books. If he is lucky he can even choose whether to play inside or outside whenever the weather is fine. The child who develops a passion for washing dolls' clothes can do this for the whole of several mornings in succession, unless the teacher interprets this as evidence of a dangerous obsession with cleanliness and tries to cure it by diverting interest elsewhere. The result of providing for the child to choose is a busy scene with the children absorbed in their self-chosen 'work' and concentrating much harder and longer than used to be thought possible at such an age.

Our willingness to allow choice to young children may, however, be a function of our belief that, since they are 'only playing', their choices are not important (which of course good preschool teachers deny). When it comes to the serious business of the primary school curriculum we reduce their choices, and from seven to eleven we prescribe a rather uniform basic core of studies for all who can cope, catering to the customer perhaps by introducing play-like activities to help the pupils master the prescribed material. A greater measure of choice is introduced at the secondary level after children have completed their exposure to the essential culture of our society.

Setting the stage for pupils to select from alternative activities might be supposed to involve every bit as much teaching skill as traditional classroom instruction in which pupils are herded from one activity to another in accordance with a planned timetable, but it constitutes a departure from the traditional role of the teacher and makes the teacher appear superficially to be less in control. In the role of customer – 'the customer is always right' – the pupil has enhanced status. His gain is not very impressive at the preschool level, however, since young children have low status anyway. But it is perhaps partly because we concede to preschool children a right to choose for themselves, and so in a measure to dictate to the teacher, that the status of the preschool teacher is low.

### Choice and commitment

The analogy between pupil and customer suggests a reason for increasing the amount of choice pupils are allowed to exercise. Goods which the customer selects for himself are more likely to be valued and used effectively than goods provided for him by a dictator however benevolent and

58

enlightened. So pupils could be expected to work harder at subjects of their own choice or in a school they want to go to; they would be likely to grumble less, and teaching would be easier and more rewarding. Carrying the analogy further, pupils might also work better if they had to pay for their instruction. Those who remain at school after the legal leaving age are in effect paying by forgoing the wages they might be earning, so they have a greater commitment to their work at school.

We might expect that schools would offer their pupils more choice in non-academic matters where teachers are not experts, for instance in matters of personal appearance. But commonly schools allow pupils less choice in these things than they are allowed outside school. Pressure, is however, growing for pupils to be allowed more choice in at least some aspects of their school lives. 'The role of the young, if they are to be adults who make their own decisions, is already to be making decisions' (Mason, 1967).

*Guidance and counselling*

We have already had occasion to refer to the guidance and counselling activities of schools. In these activities the client role of the pupil is most clearly shown. As client the pupil is receiving help or advice rather than information or qualifications. According to current counselling theory, the counsellor's role is to help the client clarify and progress towards goals of his own choosing. The reciprocal role of the pupil as client is to accept help. But the pupil is immature and his position weak. It is therefore harder for him than for an adult client to maintain his integrity in the face of subtle pressure from a counsellor, or from a teacher taking the role of counsellor. The pupil may be constrained to choose goals the counsellor considers worthy, and to adopt a line of action the counsellor judges good. And if there is clear conflict between the goals of the pupil and those of the establishment, and the

59

counsellor represents the establishment, both counsellor and client face difficulties in their role performance. The counsellor as a member of the establishment is often under pressure from the headteacher and other teachers, who misunderstand his role, to use his counselling skills to eliminate behaviour that is a nuisance to the school, and to channel pupils' ambitions in administratively convenient directions.

For the pupil the counselling situation is one in which he is denied the usual support of his classmates, exposed on his own to the full force of an adult committed to helping him, and stripped of the conventional props by which social distance between him and his teacher is usually preserved. In this situation he is invited to accept the counsellor's interpretation of his past behaviour and the counsellor's proposals for his future behaviour.

Outside the school, care is taken that counselling should be done by people who stand in no other relationship to the clients, and ordinarily counselling is undertaken only with clients who seek that kind of help. Inside the school similar safeguards are even more badly needed. From the vulnerable position of a pupil, to be required to relate to a classroom teacher as counsellor can be a threat to personal freedom. The pupil knows the teacher will look on him more favourably if he performs the client role well – if he exposes his secret feelings, and accepts the teacher's interpretation of his actions.

The teacher wanting to help a pupil is likely to move from the role of counsellor to the role of therapist, and Illich (1971) criticises this situation vehemently:

> The *teacher-as-therapist* feels authorized to delve into the personal life of his pupil in order to help him grow as a person. When this function is exercised by a custodian and preacher, it usually means that he persuades the pupil to submit to a domestication of his vision of truth and his sense of what is right.

As a component of the pupil role, the role of client-to-counsellor will never be entirely absent as long as the pupil is less mature than the teacher. The teacher of children will always be part counsellor, even part therapist, just as he is also part enemy and part missionary, part disciplinarian and part instructor. What matters is that efforts to help should be tempered by understanding of the dangers of helping, and respect for the right of the pupil to be helped towards his own goals or not to be helped at all.

Realising the problems associated with the role of teacher-as-counsellor, schools increasingly appoint full-time specialised counsellors who are freed from ordinary teaching duties and from the usual obligations of teachers to enforce the official norms. This makes it easier and safer for pupils to enter into the appropriate relationship with the counsellor.

*Conclusion*

We have noted a number of ways in which schools provide scope for choice by pupils. There are great variations in the scope for choice in different schools and at different levels of education. The principle of choice comes into conflict with the claims of the teaching profession to know best what pupils need, and the conflicting claims of pupils and teachers have somehow to be reconciled.

We have seen that there are dangers for pupils in being exposed to counselling and guidance in schools, and the dangers suggest a need for precautions to safeguard the pupils' autonomy when they are to be helped through counselling.

# 7

# The factory and the garden

He spoke wisely who said that schools were workshops of humanity, since it is undoubtedly through their agency that man really becomes man (Comenius, 1632).

In many ways education can be considered an industry. Is it an efficient industry? How can its productivity be measured? (Musgrave, 1965).

[In Russia] The needs of the state are supreme, then, and the purpose of education is clearly understood to be that of providing the necessary manpower for the economy (Carter, 1966).

In the technological society ... highly trained men replace raw materials and the factory machine as the crucial economic resource; and these men are trained through the educational institution ... (Clark, 1962).

In an investment orientation to education we are concerned above all with the relations between the resources utilized to form human competencies ... and the increments to productivity that result (Bowman, 1968).

These quotations, whether or not we agree with the ideas

expressed, exemplify a view of education which pervades a great deal of educational writing today. The analogy between a school and a factory turns up so often that we have almost ceased to be aware that it is an analogy. We speak freely of the 'product' of the public schools or the 'output' of a medical school or the 'market' for arts graduates.

Two different but related concepts of the pupil can be found in our set of quotations. According to the first concept the school can be seen as a production line turning out into society its finished product made from the raw material of the pupils' potentialities. According to the second concept the product of the school is itself regarded as a resource to be utilised by society for furthering its wealth or well-being.

Once we have noted the analogy we easily see a parallel between a school and a factory, between the entering pupil and the raw material which goes into the factory, between the leaving pupil and the finished product from the factory, and between the teacher and the factory worker. Toffler (1970) sees the school of our era as an ingenious adjunct to industrialism, using the industrial model of the factory, not only as an efficient means of mass education but also as a preview of adult working life for those destined to serve industry :

> Yet the whole idea of assembling masses of students (raw material) to be processed by teachers (workers) in a centrally located school (factory) was a stroke of industrial genius ... The schoolchild did not simply learn facts that he could use later on; he lived, as well as learned, a way of life modelled after the one he would lead in the future.

And it is easy to carry the analogy further and think of tests and examinations as part of the quality control, of dropouts as the imperfect products which are thrown on the scrap-heap, and of the return on capital outlay as a decisive factor in the allocation of resources to education.

The concept of the pupil as material to be shaped by the

63

educational processes of the school into an appropriate end-product – we could call it the 'plastic pupil' concept for short – does not give us a perspective we could properly call a role of the pupil, since pupil viewed in this way is thing, not person, and things do not have roles in the social sense. Nevertheless it is a view of the pupil that merits consideration alongside other views which acknowledge the pupil as person, so let us look at some of the important implications of this view.

*Quality control*

Measurement of the outcomes of the educational process has already been discussed in connection with the instructional role of the teacher (Chapter 3). But the same measurement is also central to the 'plastic pupil' view. Awareness of the expectation that pupils are to be processed so that they will measure up to 'quality control' standards implied by test results and examination passes is acute for teachers. It is no less acute for pupils, and in this respect pupils depart from the image of the raw material processed in a factory : material does not have feelings about its adequacy. Not only are pupils who do not pass aware of themselves as inadequate because they fall short of the standards set, but the effect on them of future processing is altered by this very awareness. It is not altered in a standard way. A few pupils are spurred to greater efforts by contemplation of their failure. Many others become less promising material because they know they have failed. This influencing of the product by labelling during processing is exacerbated by streaming, which 'to some extent *manufactures* the differences on which it is justified by teachers' (Hargreaves, 1967).

Pupils, too, may have to reinterpret past experience in the light of what happens to them. The teacher, perhaps to avoid feeling inadequate, often conveys openly or implicitly that the pupils were defective material from the beginning, and

64

not able to be formed into a product that would meet the set standards.

In a factory, all the products which pass inspection are acceptable. In a school, or in the education system as a whole, the inspection is often competitive, so that the more success-ful all the pupil's age-mates are in their performance, the less likely that pupil is to qualify. This situation rests on a some-what curious assumption, curious at least for teachers to adopt. It rests on the assumption that the material (cap-abilities of pupils) will not vary from year to year, nor will the effects of the processing (teaching), therefore standards may be kept constant by rejecting a fixed percentage of candi-dates. Such an assumption clearly reflects an absence of absolute standards, and leads us to suspect that there is some-thing more behind the examination system than an attempt to sort the products of the education process into those which are suitable for their purpose and those which are not. The something more is indeed the main purpose of testing; it is a means of allocating privilege, the privilege of further education or of entry into sought-after occupations. Thus once again the pupil is seen to be caught up in a social process that has little in common with what happens to material in a factory.

## Human rejects

Factory rejects or seconds have no hard feelings about being rejected, but human rejects from the schools are different. They seek some way to preserve their self-esteem. The sanest way to do this is to reject the system that rejects them, to preserve their own selves by discarding the values of that system.

Sometimes factory products are very hard to check for quality and the producer relies rather on making sure the material has been subjected to the right processes. There is a close parallel to this in education. Quality in the human

THE FACTORY AND THE GARDEN

product is much harder to assess than in most factory products, so we tend to rely more heavily on judgments of human quality based on the processes to which people have been exposed, a tendency which has been severely criticised by Illich (1971). He claims that the process is confused with the product: fitness for a job or for further education is judged on the basis of courses so far attended rather than competence attained.

In spite of a few undoubted similarities between the school and the factory, it seems that the 'plastic pupil' concept is not very useful, either as a description (since persons behave differently in many important respects from materials), or as a guide (since the consequences of treating pupils as things to be processed are likely to be disastrous). Only when we are limiting our attention to strictly economic aspects of education might the analogy be justified.

From the point of view of the pupil himself the analogy is even less appropriate. He does not see himself as something to be moulded or shaped, formed or processed, and for others to see him in this light is insulting to his awareness of himself as a person.

## The school as a garden

A somewhat pleasanter version of pupils-as-things is that which sees them as plants to be cultivated. Thus Wilson (1962) speaks of 'a favourable climate where the teacher can culti-vate children', and the literature on streaming is apt to refer to some pupils as 'late bloomers'. Peters (1969) describes the theory underlying the Plowden Report as based on the view that 'education is growth', from which it follows that a teacher is 'a child-grower who stands back and manipulates the environment'. This analogy fits well with the goal of 'self-actualisation', or, in modern slang, doing one's thing. In terms of such a horticultural analogy the child is to be provided with conditions which will favour his growth-from-within, interference with his own natural development being avoided or restricted to a certain amount of pruning.

Needless to say this view of the pupil is, again, not a view we could expect the pupil to share, nor do the adults who speak in these terms think of themselves as mature plants. The teacher may have an expectation that the pupils, or at least some of them, will 'blossom', but the pupils will not have expectations which could be expressed in such terms. Pupils experience themselves as acting in or on their environment rather than being nourished by it.

*Conclusion*

Thus the two versions of pupil-as-thing which we have considered underline the disjunction between the teacher and the pupil perspective. To the teacher the pupil is the object of his ministrations; to himself the pupil is the subject. The teacher sees himself as doing things to which the pupil responds, but the pupil is aware of himself as an actor to whom the teacher reacts.

# 8

## Pupils amongst their peers

'When our seven-year-old daughter used to come rushing to us excitedly and say in one breath, "What-has-a-mouth-and-can't-talk-a-river-ha-ha", of course we used to laugh, but we were laughing at her, not with her.' This father's comment points to a great gulf which separates adult from child, teacher from pupil. The pupil enjoys jokes the teacher can't share. Only his own peers can enter into many of his pleasures and anxieties. Some such insight no doubt prompted a striking comment in *New Roles for the Learner* (Mason, 1967):

> It might be wise to accept ... the need the young have of each other, and to see that it is stronger than any need they have of us.

For children of school age, the school is much the most important context for peer group relationships. Pupils in the same class spend a very great deal of time together, and they are together in a variety of settings in which their personalities are exposed very clearly to one another's scrutiny. They have opportunities to get to know one another which, for many of them, will not ever again in their lives be equalled. Some of the friendships they make at school are destined to endure for the rest of their lives.

Perhaps, then, we should pay more attention than we do to the school as a setting for peer relationships. When

68

proposals are made to 'deschool' society, this aspect of the school's social function is ignored.

*The school sets the stage*

As a peer group setting, the school determines through its arrangements for grouping pupils the circle from which pupils will choose their friends. Almost all of a school pupil's friends will be from his own school, and most from his own class. His class consists of pupils close to his own age, having similar ability, doing the same subjects, and usually drawn from much the same social class. The typical pupil probably finds it easy to make some friends when this sorting into classes has been done by the school, but the friendships some children might have formed with others of somewhat different age, ability or social class have little scope for development. There may be school rules which forbid pupils to be in any but their own classroom during breaks, for instance. Class loyalties are fostered by competition between classes, and teachers often show the pupils that they think of a class as an entity, as a good or bad, trustworthy or unreliable, satisfactory or disappointing class. Thus both the spatial arrangements and the teachers' expectations favour the development of a strong sense of belonging in a class, with 'our' room, 'our' teacher, 'our' monitors, and even 'our' nitwit and 'our' bighead. Somewhat inconsistently, the school then expects pupils who have identified with their class and come to feel at home in it to welcome a chance of promotion to a higher class, or to appreciate being removed from their classmates for special remedial work.

The school's organisation of pupils into classes and courses is, therefore, an important part of the setting in which peer group norms arise. Complex processes of differentiation, and clear boundaries which mark off the members of one school from the members of another, and the members of classes within schools, ensure that members of each school class have

69

a great deal in common with one another, and much less in common with other pupils; hence it is not surprising that divergent systems of peer group norms emerge. Some of the norms which shape the behaviour of pupils with their peers are, however, of almost universal application. Early in primary school, a pupil learns not to 'tell tales', not to 'split', not to 'blub' when hurt or punished; a boy learns to fight when challenged, to issue challenges himself when someone calls him a liar or is rude to his sister; and boys and girls learn not to be so friendly with the teacher or to turn in such good work that they are called 'teacher's pet'. At this early stage in their school career, too, pupils achieve the solidarity that enables them to have the teacher on, or to resist excessive work demands.

## Playground games

But young pupils find the fullest expression of their distinctive culture in playground games which stand apart from the adult culture surrounding them, and which are passed from one generation of school children to the next without adult intervention. Although not the only setting in which such games flourish, with universal education the school playground has become the principal setting for many games, some of which are current throughout the English-speaking world and beyond. The Opies (1969) give some examples which can be traced back in history to Greek times. Games vary from place to place, but within one school the details are rigidly fixed. A pupil coming from another school has to learn the version current in his new school.

With the games go chants and language rituals and a special vocabulary, which, as the Opies point out (1959), are useful in several ways: they give cohesion and a 'code of oral legislation' to the child society, and provide an opportunity for the children to feel secretive, daring and independent of adults.

70

The schoolchild, in his primitive community, conducts his business with his fellows by ritual declaration. His affidavits, promissory notes, claims, deeds of conveyance, receipts, and notices of resignation, are verbal, and are sealed by the utterance of ancient words which are recognized and considered binding by the whole community.

So separate is this culture from the world of older people that the Opies noted that much of it was very rapidly forgotten in early adolescence. Children who, a year before, had enthusiastically demonstrated a game, now when questioned about it 'listened to our queries with blank incomprehension'.

The games and chants reflect basic concerns of childhood: the search for order, the love of ritual, meticulous and even compulsive adherence to prescribed forms; a delight in language for its own sake, and in the nonsensical, the ridiculous and the inconsequential; satisfaction in recounting wicked deeds and a matter-of-fact treatment of sickness and death. The games themselves are often preceded by elaborate rites for allocating the players to their roles or sides, and these preliminaries may be more complicated and time-consuming than the games.

In passing we may note that the Opies' (1969) observations led them to conclude that

> when children are herded together in the playground, which is where the educationalists and the psychologists and the social scientists gather to observe them, their play is markedly more aggressive than when they are in the street or in the wild places.

But suddenly (at an age that has decreased with the arrival of organised sport, say the Opies) the child has outgrown these childish things, and the world of the adolescent opens before him. Let us now sample the secondary school culture as it has been described in some recent studies.

*Adolescent peer group norms*

At the secondary school level the influence of the peer group reaches its peak, and it is now more important than at any age before or after to do what the group does. In the school setting a pupil's behaviour is very visible to his fellow-pupils; they observe him more critically and more continuously than his teachers, and exert strong pressure on him to conform.

Below is a partial list of pupil norms for junior pupils in a school described by Inglis (1961):

A pupil is not to be seen in the company of a boy from another House.

He must not consort with older boys in the same House.

He must respond to a monitor's call of 'doul' by dropping whatever he is doing, coming on the run, and carrying out any errand assigned.

He must completely ignore local 'oicks' when they knock his hat off.

He must not appeal to a Housemaster against being beaten by a monitor (for a recognised offence).

He must correct the mistakes in his fellow-pupil's paper when papers have been exchanged for marking (instead of marking them wrong).

He must wear his jacket buttoned up (whereas older boys wore them unbuttoned).

Breaking of school rules was admired.

For boys entering the school, it was more urgent to learn the peer group norms than to learn official rules, and within a term the code had been thoroughly assimilated.

72

'Anti-squealing' norms are amongst the most widely embraced norms in the school culture, having generally the support of teachers as well as pupils. The pupils' allegiance to these norms, however, extends to situations where teachers think telling would be justified, as in a case reported by Lacey (1970) in which a pupil with a badly cut lip and swollen eye refused to name his adversary.

Even the anti-squealing norm, however, is not universally accepted, as witness one school described in Inglis's book. This school had a tale-bearing culture in which it was the done thing to report to the Head of the House behaviour seen to let the House down. The practice was known as 'showing up', and was an indication of keenness and loyalty to one's House. Pupils expected to be rewarded for this reporting of breaches.

## Academic and anti-academic subcultures

A particular secondary modern school has been described in great detail by Hargreaves (1967). Hargreaves found that the norms varied significantly from one fourth form to another. Boys in the top stream favoured hard work; regular attendance to increase the form's chance of winning the Attendance Shield; fairly conventional and tidy dress including trousers rather than jeans, and ties; and plastic cases to carry their books. They were unfavourably disposed to fighting, bad language, getting 'rowdy' when the teacher was out of the room, and copying or cheating. ('I'd tell someone how to do it, but I wouldn't show him the answer.') Thus their norms approximated those of the establishment.

The second stream boys thought the top stream boys soft and liked a class where you could 'have a giggle'. 'We don't like boys who don't mess about.' Boys were disliked if they worked hard. 'We don't like boys who answer a lot of questions' – because this might bring the lesson more quickly to the point where the teacher stopped explaining and required

73

some written work to be done. An admired pupil in this stream was a boy known for pulling faces, calling out, throwing things, and getting caned. Copying one another's work was approved. 'If a lad doesn't let you copy we call him tight.' Fights were rare but fighters had prestige. Attendance did not matter. It was normal to have dirty shoes, and wearing a tie was 'thick'. Plastic cases for books are 'not worth it, are they?'

In the lower streams the norms moved even further from the official norms of the school. The norm was not against working hard, but against working *at all*. Copying was not to simulate achievement but to soothe the teacher into thinking some work was being done. Boys even contemplated staying away from school indefinitely, 'But if you stay off six weeks like 92, it's boring'. The leading clique required its members not only to be good fighters but to go around looking for trouble. In fact the resort to violence was characteristic of low stream behaviour: 'I copy off 75 ... He couldn't stop me 'cos I'd smash him and take the book.' 'They'd take the mickey out of a lad that came in a tie.' 'I wouldn't do exams. I'd rip the paper up.' Foul language was approved. To be approved by the teacher was to be disapproved by one's classmates.

*Avoiding success*

It is interesting that the basic official norm of the school system, that achievement in school subjects is praiseworthy, is by no means accepted wholeheartedly even by the pupil groups whose norms are nearest to the official norms. This becomes apparent when schools promote achievement by encouraging competition and rewarding outstanding per-formance by official approval. Pupils may consciously moderate their achievement to conform more closely with the group. Valentine (1956) reports instances amongst bright pupils, and any class of university students is likely to contain some who can report occasions at secondary school when

74

they tried not to be best or kept their high marks secret from their classmates. Pupil norms require that at the very least a pupil with an outstanding mark should act as if it is not important.

Low stream pupils have an additional reason for avoiding high achievement: fear of promotion.

I didn't want to be top of the class. I wanted to stay where I was. That's why I stayed off [school] for the test (Hargreaves, 1967).

One widely current norm covers the attitude of pupils to school generally and to some subjects in particular. Pupils of all ages concur in taking the attitude that school attendance is an imposition, and rejoice when given a holiday or allowed out early. In taking such a view, pupils of course share an adult norm that work is necessarily tedious and holidays are naturally fun. Then again, amongst school subjects there are often agreed preferences, and pupils may vehemently contend that mathematics is terrible, while history is easy, in spite of the fact that objectively the opposite holds true for many pupils.

## Sex differences in norms

Widespread traditions of this sort may have a profound influence on subject choices and achievement. The beliefs differ somewhat with the sex of the pupils, so that girls may be prevented from performing well in mathematics and science because they accept the view that these are hard or even unsuitable for girls, while boys may waste their musical or literary talents because they regard singing and poetry as sissy or 'soft'. The need to comply with standards of masculinity or femininity is strong during this adolescent period. Stereotypes of masculine and feminine behaviour may take more extreme forms in single sex schools than in co-educational schools, where fantasies about the opposite sex are rapidly dispelled.

Different attitudes to school subjects are one manifestation of sex differences in pupil norms. Other obvious differences are to be found in fighting norms and in playing the fool. No requirement is laid on girls to stick up for themselves by fighting, and the presence of girls may even alter the requirements for boys. Girls less often play the fool. They are also less rigorously governed by the 'stiff upper lip' norm.

Interesting norms regulate the kinds of physical contact allowed between members of the same sex, and between the sexes, at different age levels. Affectionate contacts between boys are barred from an early age, but girls may hold hands or link arms. Boys achieve physical contact through some sports, and by fighting; and they engage in a great deal of jostling and shoving, which is a permitted form of contact. Between sexes, modes of contact arise at ages before typical sexual approaches are made. Boys may pull a girl's hair or snatch her ruler. Observers of girls and boys aged about fourteen travelling to school by train have reported to me that girls would frequently ruffle the hair of a smaller boy, and would initiate contact with a boy their own size by grabbing something from him and hiding it under their jacket, whence the boy was expected to retrieve it.

## Conclusion

These are just a few of the many ways in which peer group norms regulate pupil behaviour. It is clear that the norms go far beyond prescribing the behaviour of pupils amongst themselves and profoundly affect the response of pupils to the official norms of the school. In the face of peer group norms which conflict with the official norms, teachers are virtually powerless, and one of the most serious problems of today's schools can be conceptualised as the resolution of the conflict between these rival sets of norms.

# 9

## Special roles of pupils

The role of the pupil is by no means homogeneous. Expectations for the behaviour of pupils vary in a number of regular ways, some of which we shall now explore.

*Age variations in the pupil role*

In the first place the role of the pupil changes with the pupil's age. Preschool children at kindergarten are expected to be more dependent on the teacher. They may need help with shoelaces, coat buttons and aprons. They may appeal to the teacher when attacked by another child. They may need help with access to materials or with putting things away. They are expected to be less emotionally mature: they may show fear of a hedgehog or shyness towards a visitor, or lash out at a child who interferes with their block building, without being unduly censured. They are not expected to help make any group decisions, such as fixing arrangements for a trip to the fire station, although they may be permitted more freedom to make some personal decisions than older children – for example, decisions about what to paint and when to stop painting. They can ask for their creations to be admired without being called skites, and if they are young enough they can cry without being called crybabies.

But as they progress through successive stages of schooling

they meet different expectations. They cannot demand the same individual attention from their teachers. Expression of emotions is disapproved. More distant goals are prescribed. Rules are more numerous and sanctions more severe. More of the school's communications with the parents are channelled through the pupil, who comes to participate more responsibly in special occasions like sports days.

By the time the pupil reaches secondary school his parents have largely been crowded out of the scene. His school career is a matter between him and the school, and it is hard for his parents to be sure whether he has been given homework and whether he has done it. He chooses to some extent between alternative pupil subcultures, and shapes his behaviour in terms of conformity to peer group norms. Increasingly he adjusts his working behaviour to his ideas about what he will 'be' when he leaves school.

The transition from secondary to tertiary education, for those who make it, often involves a radical change in expectations which bewilders students. At university Ethel is now Miss Bradshaw. She can write her notes in purple ink in a book no-one will ever inspect, wear eyeshadow and outrageous ear-rings or bare feet and frayed jeans, and elect student representatives to attend faculty meetings. She can stay away from lectures. The university seems to consist mainly not of classrooms but of a students' union where the action is. Work is done mostly late at night in a study-bedroom in a student hostel. It is not surprising if this transition induces a kind of culture shock in a proportion of students.

*Variations between schools and classes*

A second set of variations in norms goes with the kind rather than the level of the school. There are striking differences based on the courses offered (for example, academic or 'modern'), the locality (for example inner London or a Welsh village), the administration (for example ILEA or a church board), the sex of the pupils, and many other factors. All of these factors contribute in important ways to the particular norms of the school – what clothes the pupils wear, what sports they play, what library books they read, how they address their teachers, how much homework they are given, their language and speech, what punishments are meted out to them. When schools of different countries are compared, the variations may be greater still. Only the skeleton of the institution we call 'school' is the same.

Even within a school there may be marked variations in the expectations for different sections of the pupils. Hargreaves (1967) reports that pupils and teachers had very different expectations for boys in different streams. A teacher was investigating a noise in the corridor:

> 'Who are you lot?' he cried. '3B, sir,' came the reply. 'You sound more like 1E than 3B!' was the master's crushing retort.

On one form blackboard Hargreaves found the notice: 'We must always remember to behave as an A class.' The allocation of teachers followed the streaming system, the best teachers being assigned to the top streams, so that differences in achievement and commitment to work were accentuated further.

*Positions of responsibility*

Besides these widespread variations based on the educational setting, there are other variations based on special positions occupied by selected pupils in most schools. Many special positions rest on seniority. Privileges may be accorded to upper school pupils, or prefects may be selected from this group. Positions of seniority or authority are often marked by special dress or a special badge, and sometimes by exemption from wearing school uniform and from other

79

requirements such as bringing notes to explain absences.

Hargreaves called attention to the way in which prefects were selected in the school he studied. They were drawn largely though not quite exclusively from the top two streams.

Teachers usually either choose the prefects themselves or exercise a power of veto over the choice of the pupils. Teachers prefer to appoint moderately studious pupils with some prowess (in boys' schools) in prestigious school sports (not, say, weightlifting or table tennis). Those appointed should be committed to the establishment, not critical of it, and able to influence others towards conformity with school rules. In fact the prefect role is principally to exercise delegated authority by enforcing the official norms of the school. If prefects perform their role faithfully, the teachers are released from an unpleasant and unrewarding part of their duties. Prefects usefully supplement the discipline of the teachers because they are more often on the spot when certain breaches of the rules occur, for instance failure to wear correct uniform when travelling to and from school. Moreover, prefects have access to methods of enforcement unavailable to teachers. They may even use physical force or the threat of it in circumstances where this would not be condoned for teachers. Hence the comment of an ex-pupil: 'There never used to be trouble about the pupils doing what the prefects told them to because they [the teachers] mostly chose members of the first fifteen.'

Not surprisingly some pupils identify with the rank and file of pupils against the establishment and prefer not to become prefects, while many others resent the exercise of the role by their schoolmates. The role of prefect is in some respects intermediate between that of the teacher and the pupil. It resembles that of the foreman, who is intermediate between the boss and the worker. Levinson (1959) says that the foreman's situation 'tends to evoke feelings of social marginality, mixed identifications, and conflicting tendencies'

80

leading to role dilemmas; and some prefects are aware of similar problems.

The prefect, however, gains privileges which may compensate for his added responsibilities. He has extra prestige, and is treated by teachers as a more adult person. The existence of such a category tends to diminish the barrier between staff and pupils.

Amongst prefects, one is singled out as head prefect, on much the same criteria as for prefectship generally. This one is expected to show leadership qualities in greater measure, and to be able to hold the allegiance of a group of prefects. The head prefect is a public figure, and has on occasion to appear before the whole school, and members of other schools and outsiders as well. He (or she) is expected to make a good impression when representing the school in public. The school must be able to count on him to dress unexceptionably, to behave in a dignified and correct way, and to speak clearly and confidently. Should this person be so indiscreet as to be caught breaking school rules – drinking, smoking, or damaging school property for instance – his misdemeanour will be very seriously regarded and he may be demoted.

One school of thought claims that leadership such as that of prefect should be shared amongst pupils as widely as possible on the grounds that latent leadership qualities are widely distributed but remain undeveloped if pupils are not called on to exercise them. Kipling's Stalky and Co. is about three boys who were too exuberant to be made prefects but had qualities of leadership the school largely failed to harness. Schools continue in the main to play safe and select for prefectship pupils who already show the qualities sought by the teachers, rather than to take the risk of appointing pupils initially less suitable in the hope that they will be changed by trying to meet the demands of their roles.

Alongside the prefect system schools commonly have a system of sports captains, who may occupy general leadership positions or be captains of particular teams. They too must present a favourable image on their school's behalf, but this must be combined with special proficiency in one or more sports, and some organising ability, so that they can deploy the skills of their teams to advantage. In some schools they have, amongst the pupils at least, even greater prestige than head prefects.

Then there are often class captains or class representatives, usually elected by the pupils. Their role is to represent their class on certain occasions such as the presentation of trophies won by the class, and perhaps to convey decisions from class meetings to teachers or from teachers to class meetings. This role is considerably enhanced if the school has a school council, a form of organisation that is growing in popularity and has replaced the prefect system in some schools. Members of school councils perform very different roles in different schools. A few schools allow pupils a genuine share in educational decisions, but most limit the function of the council to certain peripheral areas which may include the conduct of some social functions. Most also reserve the right of the teachers to veto any pupil proposal. A few insist that the headteacher attend all meetings, and allow in the agenda only items approved by the headteacher, thus effectively stultifying the participation of pupils. Systems like this, paying only lip service to pupil participation, are described by Kelley (1962) as 'adult shams'. Kelley describes a United States experiment in which pupils were given a real share in the government of the school. The pupils consisted of a motley collection of fourteen- to eighteen-year-olds mainly, many of them rejects or drop-outs from the regular schools. They attended one day a week, often very unwillingly, and fights between teachers and pupils were not uncommon. An experiment in self-government was begun as a desperate measure to counter the hostility of the pupils. Each class had a president and secretary elected by the pupils (800 presidents and secretaries all told). These officers took ideas for improving the school from the monthly class council meetings to a group meeting which either accepted each idea and sent it forward, or rejected it and sent it back with the reason for rejecting it. Resolutions finally reached the School Council, and, if accepted there, were sent to the principal, who in turn either implemented them or wrote a full explanation of the problem which prevented their implementation. This went back to the class which had originated the proposal. Such a procedure establishes a markedly different role for the pupil and could in time give rise to many other changes in the pupil's role.

Some even more specialised positions of responsibility are common in schools. Selected pupils may become class monitors or librarians or bell-ringers. There may be a roster of pupils to prepare staff morning tea and wash up afterwards, and perhaps in a mixed school only the girls will be put on this roster. On the other hand, boys and not girls may be assigned to milk duty. School policy in such matters can reinforce sex roles, or, instead, disregard sex in the allocation of duties. In deciding its policy the school faces a characteristic dilemma, whether to reflect the norms of the community, or whether to base its norms on an ideal society different from that in which the school subsists: in this case, whether to adopt certain principles of women's liberation before or after they are established in the world outside the school.

Pupils are often given a temporary role of messenger. It is usually regarded as a privilege to go on an errand for a teacher. Hargreaves (1967) reports an interesting instance in which he gave an errand to a boy the teacher considered unreliable:

The teacher turned to me and said, 'You don't want to send him if you want to get those stamps today,' and asked another boy to run the errand. Derek, who seemed both surprised and pleased by my request now began to scowl. When I insisted that Derek should go for me, Derek looked at me and said, 'Are you sure?'

This incident illustrates the special expectations associated with the messenger role, and it also illustrates the way in which the allocation of special roles can be used by teachers to convey and to reinforce their assessments of pupil character.

Some special duties are assigned to less able pupils in order not to interfere with the studies of the bright pupils. Messenger duties may fall into this category. Hargreaves (1967) reports an expectation by some teachers that milk duty should be assigned to boys in the lower streams in order not to interfere with the examination prospects of the brighter boys. Thus once again we see pupils being fitted into roles which accentuate the differences already existing between them.

*Roles based on academic status*

Besides roles in which special responsibility is a principal ingredient, there are other roles in which the focus is on special merit or demerit. The school dux achieves a status which does not depend on popularity with fellow-pupils or teachers and does not necessarily involve the incumbent in special responsibility. The position of dux is a symbol of the school's concern with academic excellence. Substantial prizes are often awarded as a mark of this status, and there may be a special honours board for their names.

At the other end of the scale are positions of very low academic status occupied by the least able pupils. 'Dunce' is a position no longer formally assigned, but it used to be common to single out some hapless pupil, separate him from his classmates in a special seat, and even make him wear a dunce's cap as a stigma. It is interesting that this institutional response to poor pupil performance has been abandoned mainly because of current doctrine that poor performance is 'not the child's fault' – he cannot help his lack of aptitude so should not be penalised for it. Yet the same argument in

84

reverse might suggest that the dux should not be rewarded for being gifted, since his aptitude is not his own doing.

Without being stigmatised as 'dunces', pupils whose work is poor are still today labelled 'backward' and assigned to special classes or to special groups within their class, and given less demanding work. Thus labelled, some may become backward even if the label was originally misapplied.

*Cock of the school*

Pupils have value systems of their own which give rise to some special roles. An example is that of 'cock' held by the boy who is supreme as a fighter. This supremacy need not be established by actually defeating all potential aspirants, as Hargreaves (1967) showed. It is enough that the pupils believe he could win. The cock in the school Hargreaves studied attracted a mixture of fear and resentment from the other pupils, so that the position although one of high prestige was not one of maximum popularity. Sensitive to this, some potential aspirants were deterred from challenging the ruling cock out of unwillingness to lose popularity.

*Relations with headteachers*

The pupil role changes when the pupil is relating to different teachers on the staff and to other non-teaching members of the school staff. The pupil's relationship to the headteacher often calls for very different behaviour from that appropriate with his class teacher. The headteacher may establish a remote and powerful image as supreme disciplinarian to whom pupils are sent when ordinary punishments are deemed insufficient, a person before whom a pupil trembles even when he knows of no wrong he has done, a person whose sanctum is to be approached on tiptoe and in accordance with an awesome ritual. Pupils avoid confrontation with such a being, and if impelled into his presence they display extreme deference and a suitable mixture of anxiety and penitence. On the other hand some headteachers adopt the role of friend and counsellor and specialise in getting recalcitrant pupils to bare their inner motives, then give them a talking-to in a fatherly manner. With this kind of headteacher a pupil feels obligated to produce an acceptable reason for his lapse and to be apologetic and grateful for not being punished.

Behaviour towards a teacher other than one's class teacher is generally more distant and more wary. Towards a caretaker or tuckshop proprietor it is often in order to be more friendly and familiar than towards a teacher, although some caretakers succeed in striking terror into the hearts of pupils.

## Conclusion

Pupils are adept at learning the variations in behaviour which these diverse relationships require. It is clear that schools supply quite a rich variety of slots for pupils of varying age, sex, intelligence and personality. As pupils come by accident or design to fit into particular slots, they tend to develop the appropriate lines of behaviour. Their school careers are profoundly influenced by the slots into which they fit, and their personalities may bear the marks of their school careers for the rest of their lives.

# 10

## The rule-breakers

Along with the existence of any rule goes the possibility of breaking it. We are now to take a look at the pupils who break the rules and come to be 'deviants'.

Isolated infringements of norms are committed by everyone frequently without any important social consequences. Something more than the mere breaking of a rule is needed for a person to become a deviant. What is this something more?

Deviance in the sociological sense is behaviour which contravenes rules and attracts disapproval in consequence. But to call a person a deviant is to imply that he *characteristically* behaves deviantly, or is prone to act deviantly. When the deviant label is applied to a person there is a transition from deviant act to deviant character. How easily the transition takes place depends on many factors: the deviant act or acts must be 'visible' or able to be noticed, and someone must in fact notice; the behaviour must be serious enough or frequent enough to warrant attention; and there must be no apparent excuse.

The kinds of pupil behaviour officially recognised as deviant usually depend on categories set up and applied by the teachers. Teachers (influenced at times by pressures from outside the school) determine what constitutes an offence, whether speaking at the wrong time or being in the wrong place or failing to do work which has been set or being

87

insolent. New teachers have to learn the definitions of school crimes from experienced teachers, unless they formerly attended a very similar school themselves. Pupils have to learn the definitions from the teachers and from other pupils.

### Labelling by teachers

When he is versed in the school's interpretation of pupil behaviour the teacher can apply recognised labels like 'backward', 'under-achiever', 'insecure', 'maladjusted', 'deprived', 'emotionally unstable'. Teachers are relatively knowledgeable in applying labels related to academic performance, such as 'under-achiever'. They are not nearly so well-equipped when it comes to labels like 'disturbed', 'emotionally unstable' or 'culturally deprived' (which, however, they freely use), so there is likely to be a greater element of unreliability in the application of these labels.

The pupil who is unfavourably labelled is in effect assigned a deviant role, and once this role has been assigned expectations are set up that the deviant behaviour will continue. Such expectations are communicated not only to the pupil but to teacher colleagues, and often, by means of records which follow a pupil from school to school, to the pupil's future teachers as well. To return to normality is then very hard, and probably requires either specially meticulous and conspicuous conformity with the rules for a long time or a complete change of context to escape from the unwanted reputation. It is usually much easier to accept the label and conform to the deviant role. The pupil thus becomes the person he is labelled as.

This can happen whether the labeller was a competent judge or not; and it can happen whether the labelling was hostile ('fool', 'lout') or intended as a basis for help ('dyslexic', 'educationally retarded').

*Emergence of subcultures*

Accepting the label is made easier for the pupil if there are others with the same label so that they can form a group with common problems. The group may then proceed to develop solutions to some of the problems the members share. One solution could be to establish a separate value system in terms of which the behaviour stigmatised by the dominant culture becomes approved by the group. Thus a subculture may arise in which hard work, good results, obedience to teachers, and conformity to school rules are despised, and cheating, dodging work, playing up and defying authority are admired. Another solution could be to develop techniques for getting away with one's misdeeds, by escaping detection or reducing the severity of the punishment. Thus an anti-academic subculture can offer pupils knowledge of places where teachers are unlikely to catch them smoking, ways of passing messages in class with impunity, sophisticated methods of cheating, and devices for making the cane or the strap hurt less.

Once a subculture is established, pupils can acquire deviant labels such as 'trouble-maker' or 'lout' simply by associating with other pupils who belong in the subculture, or by dressing as they dress. The subculture tends to build its own more or less coherent value system which often systematically contradicts the dominant set of values. It may offer its members a complete way of life – language and speech, dress, locations, recreation, interests. Hargreaves (1967) describes in great detail a lower stream culture in a secondary modern school, which he calls 'delinquescent'. Amongst a substantial number of the lower stream pupils he found that theft, for instance, was acceptable :

> 'It's not wrong to nick things out of shops. They've got more money than us.'

But, as in many other subcultures, the dominant norms were also recognised as having some validity:

'Once I leave school and start work I'm going to be dead careful ... You see more kids at school pinching than grown ups. ...'

Hargreaves noted truancy as a feature of the deviant subculture. He also noted distinctive patterns of dress, including peer group pressure to grow hair long. He described a conflict in which long-haired school leavers were told that the head would not give them a reference and they would find it hard to get jobs. Even this threat was ineffective against the group norms, for 'group norms were much more attractive and compelling than teacher expectations'. The pupil's identity comes to be closely linked with his group membership, and conformity to group norms is necessary to protect this identity. Deviant behaviour in such a situation has to be understood not as *refusal to conform* to the norms of the dominant culture, but as *insistence on conforming* to the norms of the subculture. This kind of slavish conformity is less necessary for a pupil who feels himself liked and valued, so building self-confidence and self-respect will lessen the need to adhere to norms which defy official standards.

Hargreaves described the diversity of norms in the school he studied in terms of a simple gradation from official-academic to delinquescent anti-academic. Clark and Trow (1965) studying student subcultures at the college level in the United States described four subcultures. One was the academic subculture, and this alone was compatible with the official cultural goals of the educational institution. The other three – the vocational subculture, narrowly concerned with getting job skills and qualifications, the 'collegiate' which put the social life of the college first, and the non-conformist – were all in some measure opposed to the official culture. Students who identified with one of these three subcultures were therefore behaving deviantly in terms of the expectations the college sets up that its students will devote themselves first and foremost to the pursuit of knowledge for its own sake.

Because they provide such convenient group settings, where deviants can join forces against the establishment, schools facilitate the growth of alternative subcultures with entrenched traditions which teachers find it hard to change. Links with the community outside the school, with social class, area of residence, and vocational expectations, further consolidate the subcultural norms. Some pupils find themselves identifying with a particular school subculture from the outset of their school careers. Others choose from the available identities the one which best fits their family and social class norms and their experience of success or failure in school. In this they are abetted by the labels applied by the teachers and by the streaming or grouping systems in the school. Streaming progressively differentiates the committed and successful pupils from the uncommitted and unsuccessful, so that a process tentatively begun in the early secondary school years gains momentum and quickly produces groups with markedly divergent values. Cicourel and Kitsuse (1971) describe the process in these terms:

The school system may be conceived as an organization which produces, in the course of its activities, a variety of adolescent careers including the delinquent.

In the production of such careers the labelling processes are begun by the teachers, perhaps with the assistance of educational and other tests designed to help the teacher identify pupils who are retarded, socially immature, handicapped, emotionally unstable, friendless or otherwise disadvantaged. (Those who are troublesome or wicked are identified without the aid of objective measurement.) The teachers are assisted not only by tests but by psychologists and guidance personnel. The pupils themselves and also their

91

parents often take some part. Talked to by a teacher, head-teacher, or counsellor, a pupil or parent produces information that is added to the file and becomes part of the damaging evidence: 'mother can't cope', 'father ineffective', 'delinquent older brother', 'bed-wetter', 'early feeding problems' – such comments are used to confirm and explain deviance and to exonerate the school. They serve to strengthen the expectation that the pupil will behave deviantly.

Deviant subcultures in schools provide roles for some of the pupils the schools account deviant, but Lacey (1970) notes that *extreme* deviants from the official culture may be rejected even by the deviating subgroup, and may find their position untenable. If they do find a niche for themselves it is likely to carry very low status.


*The class clown*

A few of the more extreme deviants may find a niche in one or other of the highly specialised individual roles that are common amongst school pupils. One such special role is that of class clown, the one who by common consent does amusing, slightly off-beat things to entertain his fellow-pupils.

How does a pupil come to occupy such a position? Not, it would seem, by imitation, since a class usually has only one such character and he could not have had a model for his behaviour. Is there as it were a vacancy in a social group for a clown as there is a vacancy for a leader, so that the functioning of the group tends to call forth a character to fill the role? This would suggest that it serves some useful purpose for the group to have someone occupying this position. In the seriousness and monotony of the classroom light relief may be highly valued.

The enthusiasm of pupils for anything that gives them an excuse to laugh is illustrated by Hines (1968) in the following incident, when the teacher had made a very feeble joke:

The class roared out again, tossing their heads back and scraping their chairs, banging their desk lids and thumping the backs and arms of any boy within range: using the joke as a mere excuse to cause havoc.

If there is to be hilarity the teacher prefers the jokes to be his own. The pupils on the other hand welcome any joke. Lacey (1970) describes ways in which grammar school boys played the fool: 'a boy might stretch so hard as to fall out of his desk, another accidentally punch the one in front as he put his hand up'. Given pupils who are on the look-out for an excuse to laugh, the teacher is understandably wary of behaviour that can be interpreted as funny, but finds it difficult to control, since it is hard to punish pupils for laughing or raising a laugh, without seeming harsh and humourless.

The role of class clown may be assigned as a result of behaviour not originally intended to be funny – a howler or a clumsy act. Finding he has raised a laugh a pupil may discover a claim to recognition that he may not have achieved in other ways. He may find it more rewarding to be laughed at than ignored. So the behaviour is worth repeating, the class enjoys the excuse to laugh, and the role is assigned.

When occupied willingly the position of the clown involves some daring, since as we have seen teachers are not apt to appreciate attempts by pupils to make each other laugh. Originality is an asset to the clown, but indiscriminate originality is a threat to institutional routines, so the clown's particular form of creativity is not officially approved.

Conditions which increase the need of the group for light relief will encourage clowning. It will be more likely to occur when boredom is at a peak; when seriousness is expected but not rigidly enforced (say towards the end of a tedious lesson rather than in an examination); and when there is an appreciative audience – not when the pupil is alone with the teacher. Typical clowning behaviour involves quite trivial acts which are funny because the audience wants them to be

93

funny : the pupil who is sent out of the room by a thoroughly exasperated teacher towards the end of a long arithmetic lesson on a hot afternoon for 'accidentally' falling out of his seat pauses in the doorway behind the teacher's back, waves to the class and says 'Toodle-oo'. The class titters delightedly.

Sometimes the role of the clown is acquired by a pupil who would much prefer (initially at least) to remain a nonentity. Such a pupil may be better described as the class butt. Lacey (1970) describes the behaviour of a boy who was laughed at for making mistakes that other boys could make with impunity, and incited by the other boys to break rules, then deserted and left to take the consequences. His eagerness to be 'one of the boys' made him vulnerable to this treatment.

On occasion the entertainment is turned on by the class as a group, the teacher being the butt. There are ritual occasions for this kind of entertainment, the most obvious being the first of April. On this day it is traditional to hide the chalk and the cane, arrange booby-traps, and play verbal tricks, and the teacher is supposed to respond by noticing and being suitably surprised or taken aback but not angry. To act as if nothing has happened is 'out of character' for the teacher's temporary role as butt.

The various disruptions which result from funny incidents, whether originating with the teacher or the pupils, present a transition problem when it is time to start being serious again. The teacher needs well-understood cues to convey to the pupils at the right moment that the entertainment is over.

### The bully

The class clown, though he is a thorn in the teacher's flesh, has the approval of his fellow-pupils, without perhaps a great deal of prestige. The class butt is rather used than approved, and certainly lacks prestige. There are other deviant behaviour types that are disapproved by pupils and teachers alike. Such

94

a type is the bully. Pupil norms as well as more general societal norms discriminate carefully between approved fighting and disapproved fighting. Approval of fighting varies with the age of the pupil, the traditions of the school, and the sub-culture within the school, but where it is approved the norms closely regulate the way of challenging and accepting a challenge and the tactics which may be used in the fight. The bully is one who breaks some of the rules, especially one who dominates those who are smaller and weaker than himself by violence or the threat of violence. Hence a boy may more easily acquire the label of bully if he is bigger than his classmates, or gets around with younger and smaller boys, and if he responds to frustration by becoming aggressive, and has not internalised the group norms which specify legitimate fighting behaviour.

*The swot*

It is implicit in our discussion of deviant behaviour up to this point, that behaviour can be designated as deviant only when we have indicated whose norms are being violated. The existence of rival sets of norms in a school makes it possible for behaviour which conforms to one set of norms to be deviant in terms of a rival set. Thus in terms of the pupil culture the conspicuously good pupil, the one who embodies all the official virtues, may be classified as a deviant character. He may attract unfavourable labels from his fellow-pupils – 'swot', 'crawler', 'goody-goody', 'teacher's pet'. It is easy to understand the origin of this disapproval. A better-than-average performance by one member of a group is threatening to the other members because it makes their own performance seem inadequate by comparison. Unfavourable labels for conspicuously good performance are avoided by most pupils, but it is curious that an occasional very bright pupil is labelled 'Professor' by his classmates and treated with affection rather than disapproval. To achieve this status amongst his peers instead of being rejected for his brilliance, the pupil should appear incapable of suppressing his mental powers, entirely unconcerned about the teacher's approval, and perhaps endearingly inadequate in some other way – absentminded, or clumsy. Such a pupil does not expose the lack of dedication of his fellows because he is somehow unique and does not invite comparison.

## Uses of deviance

The emergence of types, including deviant types, amongst the members of a group serves a number of useful purposes (Cohen, 1966). The deviant group member tests, clarifies and demonstrates the behavioural limits imposed by the norms, without risk to the conformers. He is often instrumental in changing the norms: long hair for boys becomes acceptable only through defiance of the standards by some bold individuals. Even as a counter to boredom deviant behaviour could sometimes be justified, and pressure to assume the role of clown or cheat or truant may come from the need for excitement and risk-taking.

## Conclusion

In conclusion, deviant behaviour in schools is a very important field of study if the role of the pupil is to be understood. We have seen that deviant behaviour has to be studied both as an individual phenomenon and also as a characteristic of certain subcultures. To be effective, the control of deviance must take into account the fact that deviant behaviours are often embedded in subcultures. The task of the school may then be to find a way to operate within the subculture rather than against it.

We should note that the labelling processes which establish some pupils as deviants are likely to impinge differently on children from different backgrounds. Middle-class parents for a number of reasons are better able to protect their children from the adverse effects of deviant labels than working-class parents, who may accept the labels and intentionally or unintentionally confirm their children in deviant roles.

# 11

## The role of the miscreant

The following extract is taken from *A Kestrel for a Knave* (Hines, 1968). A boy who has committed the offence of dropping off to sleep during the singing of the Lord's Prayer stands silent, red-faced, head bowed, before the teacher.

'And get your head up lad! Or you'll be falling asleep again!'
Billy lifted his face. ...
'You were asleep, weren't you? ... Well? Speak up, lad!'
'I don't know, Sir.'
'Well I know. You were fast asleep on your feet. Weren't you?'
'Yes, Sir.'
...
'Were you tired, lad?'
'I don't know, Sir.'
'Don't know? You wouldn't be tired if you'd get to bed at night instead of roaming the streets at all hours up to mischief!'
'No, Sir.'

Although this is a fictional account, we recognise only too well the roles of the performers, outraged teacher and recalcitrant pupil. The passage illustrates several general

98

characteristics of the situation of the pupil caught out in a misdemeanour.

In the first place the pupil can't win. He is repeatedly placed in the situation of having to say something that he knows will be taken to incriminate him further. In answer to the question, 'Were you tired?', if he says 'Yes, Sir' he will be bawled out for his night-time activities, as subsequent events show. If he says 'No, Sir' he will be bawled out for going to sleep when he isn't tired. If he does not answer he is likely to make the teacher madder and invite further equally unanswerable questions. In the circumstances 'I don't know' seems the best available choice, although it lays him open to the charge of being a moron.

In the second place, we can note the very fine line which divides the inoffensive from the offensive behaviour. Billy hangs his head, and the teacher shouts at him to hold his head up. Had he begun by holding his head up and looking the teacher in the face and speaking up, he might have run an even greater risk of further offending the teacher, for he might have seemed impenitent. There is possibly an intermediate head position and loudness of speech which would not have invoked wrath, but Billy has not yet mastered the niceties of the required behaviour, although he shows himself familiar with the general expectations pertaining to the miscreant role.

Next we can note the non-committal nature of Billy's replies. Billy avoids contradicting the teacher. He tries to agree with him, as his final 'No, Sir' shows. We do not for a moment imagine Billy is really expressing his own opinion about his night life. He is simply giving the reply appropriate to his situation.

Although it is generally sensible to agree with the teacher in this kind of situation, there are times when it would be unwise to do so. Consider this instance from the same book: the teacher is about to cane some boys who were smoking.

'I know what you're thinking now, you're thinking, why doesn't he get on with it and let us go, instead of standing there babbling on? That's what you're thinking isn't it, MacDowall?'

'No, Sir.'

'Oh yes it is. I can see it in your eyes . . .'

Now, in spite of the form of this interchange MacDowall divines correctly that the teacher does *not* expect him to agree, that it would be unwise to agree, so he says 'No, Sir' and the teacher carries on as he had intended to carry on. 'Yes, Sir' would have outraged the teacher and further intensified his attack.

Finally we may note that Billy makes no attempt to explain or justify his behaviour. His experience has already taught him that it is unwise to explain even if the teacher demands an explanation. An enraged teacher can turn any explanation into an occasion for further recrimination. Experienced miscreants therefore often say as little as possible. A stubborn (in the teacher's view) refusal to answer may, however, incense the teacher further, so it is generally best for the pupil to say 'Yes, Sir' or 'No, Sir' unless he is so terrified that he is in danger of selecting the wrong one. In the army in a like situation it is held to be an appropriate strategy to stand at attention and say simply 'Sir!' thus avoiding the necessity of choosing the right alternative.

## Explanations and apologies

Some situations arise in which an attempt to explain is in order. In these cases it is important to offer the right sort of explanation. The teacher may want not to reprimand or punish the pupil, preferring a more friendly role, and a suitable explanation or apology permits the teacher to avoid being punitive. Goffman (1972) calls these explanations 'accounts', and discusses the forms that accounts can take.

The offender may for instance offer an account by claiming that the act did not occur; that he was not the perpetrator; that circumstances existed which made the act in effect different from what it appeared to be; that he did not intend or foresee the consequences; that the act was intended as a joke; that the actor was not fully responsible for his acts; or that although indefensible his act was a brief lapse rather than a symptom of permanent moral defect. If the miscreant is able to give what Goffman calls a good account, this has the effect of making him less blameworthy and may reduce or eliminate the penalty.

The timing of an explanation may be important, and it is sometimes best to save one's account until the wrath of the person offended has subsided a little and he is in a better mood both to listen and to forgive.

Accounts are commonly coupled with apologies, and Goffman's (1972) analysis of the apology is very pertinent to an understanding of the role of pupil as miscreant. An individual apologising, he says, splits himself into two parts, the part that broke the rule and the part that affirms the rule – the blameworthy part and the blaming part. A comprehensive apology includes a number of elements which can be summed up as follows: unhappiness at having acted so, repudiation of the wrong way of acting and of himself for acting wrongly, acceptance of the right way and acknowledgment of that way as a future standard, an expression of intention to conform to that standard henceforth, and an offer to perform acts of penance and restitution.

Good apologies, like good accounts, appease the person offended and may reduce the penalty or get the offender excused. Some specific rules for pupils for conduct when caught offending include the following:

Adopt a dejected stance.
Look sorry, apprehensive and unhappy. On no account smile.

Never interrupt the teacher, even if he is wrong.

Don't explain until or unless a genuine invitation to do so is issued.

When explaining, be sparing.

Meet the teacher's eyes only reluctantly. Don't stand up too straight, but don't slouch.

Don't put your hands in your pockets.

Don't turn your head away or look past the teacher.

Don't blame someone else.

Speak timidly and hesitantly rather than confidently and fluently.

Don't challenge the validity of the rule, or the teacher's right to enforce it.

It is better to take the view that your act is a surprising and regrettable lapse rather than a habitual act in which you have been unluckily caught out.

Naturally no one type of excuse is appropriate to all occasions. One could hardly explain when caught smoking behind the toilets that one did not mean to do it, but one might claim that falling out of one's desk and making everyone laugh was an accident. One could hardly claim that arriving late for school was not in fact arriving late, but one might (perhaps unwisely) claim that 'I didn't kick him, I just pushed him with my foot'. So the pupil has to learn not just a single response sequence but a whole repertoire of alternative sequences from which to select the best for a particular set of circumstances, and he must be adept at modifying his behaviour to the ever-changing exigencies of the situation.

A suitable apology not only softens the teacher's wrath, it returns the initiative to the teacher and permits him to close the incident if he so wishes. He can be kind and forgiving instead of angry and critical if this suits him. Care is needed in bringing an incident to a close. An offender should show gratitude and relief if he has been excused. To turn away too soon, or stop looking and sounding sorry, or walk away whistling, discredits the performance. On the other hand the pupil will want to convey to any fellow-pupils who are present that he is not as abject as he seems, so a nice balance will need to be achieved.

## Receiving punishment

If the offender's account and apology do not get him excused, further norms govern his behaviour when punished. Corporal punishment when used is to be accepted without flinching but there should be some subtle signal to the teacher that it does hurt and self-control is being exercised. The offender might bite his lip, tense his muscles, or hold or rub the sore place. A too convincing show of not being hurt would expose the pupil and his fellow pupils to an intensification of the teacher's efforts. Finally, the pupil should depart with, as it were, his tail between his legs, looking subdued.

The pupil culture includes traditional procedures for making punishment less arduous, although astute teachers are up with the play. Pupils may rescue the lines they have written from the waste paper basket to be reused. They may hold their hands in ways that are supposed to make the cane hurt less. They adopt devices such as Williamson describes (Inglis, 1961):

> As an insurance against pain, part of an old leather satchel was sewn to the inside seat of my knickerbockers. Did the wallops resound somewhat alarmingly loud? My tears flowed the more abundantly, my face expressed despairing contrition, the more the stings failed to penetrate my shield.

## Requests

Somewhat akin to apologies are certain requests which, if granted, permit the pupil to act in ways that would otherwise

103

have been forbidden. Successful use of requests requires the pupil to judge accurately when permission is likely to be granted. It is a tactical error to ask permission and be refused when one intends to carry out an act anyway. It is obviously an advantage to have permission to leave school early if there is any danger of being caught; but once permission has been sought and denied, the penalty for being caught leaving early is likely to be much greater, and the teacher has also been alerted to notice the pupil's departure. Pupils often calculate their chances very accurately in such situations.

Some requests, and for that matter some offences, are used by pupils as indirect means of gaining attention. Moreover the whole fabric of routines for handling offences is designed partly with the spectator in mind. These routines thus serve latent functions in shaping relationships and interactions at the same time as they further their manifest function of maintaining and restoring recognised roles. Playing to the gallery is a conspicuous feature of pupil behaviour especially when there is a pupil subculture that is opposed to the official culture, and this is one reason why it is so often remarked that troublesome pupils on their own are reasonable and manageable, whereas in a group they are out of reach of the teacher's efforts to induce compliance.

### Avoiding detection

We have been considering the expectations that influence the behaviour of pupils when they have been caught out in a misdemeanour. But not all infringements follow such a course. Some are never discovered, or, becoming known, are ignored. Since it is a general aim of most pupils to avoid unnecessary trouble, pupils learn to conceal their misdeeds as far as possible. They may practise talking without moving their lips, choose the moment when the teacher's back is turned to pass a note or launch a dart, simulate earnest attention, keep a swot book handy for the moment when the suspicious teacher asks them to bring out the book they are reading, and generally preserve a front of unflustered innocence. Some pupils are much more skilful than others at surreptitious activity, and some manage to be much less conspicuous in ordinary infringements in which almost all pupils frequently engage, such as talking when they are not supposed to.

### Managing as a miscreant

The teacher's expectations also enter into the situation so that he notices the misdeeds of pupils he thinks of as trouble-makers, and fails to notice when 'good' pupils misbehave. Thus the pupils who are most often in trouble are not always those who infringe most often. Those who lack personal charm, or who are clumsy or careless in their efforts at concealment, or poor at their work, or aggressive when apprehended, quickly acquire a reputation which places them under continual suspicion so that in any large-scale disorder they are the ones who are noticed and singled out for punishment. They may even acquire files which follow or precede them from class to class and from school to school, and warn each successive teacher what to expect. Teachers naturally prefer to ascribe mischief to known troublemakers rather than to 'good' pupils. It is disturbing to have one's classification of pupils into goodies and baddies confounded.

Lacey (1970) relates an instructive incident in which a teacher, Wilkins, insists that the boy who made 'a large raspberry noise' as the teacher entered the room should own up:

At the end of the lesson Hodge came forward and admitted to making the noise. Wilkins was shocked and upset. He kept saying, 'I can't understand it. Hodge isn't that sort of boy. I could understand Morris, or even Larch, but not Hodge.'

When later in the day Hodge apologised and explained that

105

the noise had been intended for another boy, Wilkins was relieved and pleased, and commented: 'I knew Hodge wouldn't do something like that purposely.' Thus teachers prefer to impute good motives to 'good' pupils and bad motives to 'bad' pupils.

It is important for a pupil who wants to create a good impression to learn appropriate ways of being inconspicuous about some of his actions, and to learn a suitable repertoire of behaviour for occasions when he is apprehended. It has been suggested that one of the serious disabilities under which working-class children labour is an inadequate repertoire of behaviours which might keep them out of trouble or minimise the consequences when they offend. One of the reasons why girls are often considered less troublesome than boys may be simply that they are better at avoiding apprehension and better at being penitent when they are caught out.

We are writing as though pupils who misbehave turn on a calculated act in order to influence the course of subsequent events. This may not always be so. They may slip so easily into the role of offender-caught-out that they are not consciously acting a part. Yet it is in this aspect of their relationship with teachers that they are most likely to be aware that they are acting a part. There is a distance between them and their role. In the miscreant role behaviour they agree with the teacher, avoid a defiant mien, sound penitent, and submit to punishment. As soon as the teacher is out of sight and earshot they discard the role and become 'themselves', justifying their behaviour and perhaps affirming their intention to persist in it. Their out-of-earshot expressions of defiance towards the teacher may be part of another role, pupils-against-teachers, but this is a role which is closer to the self of the pupil.

It says a great deal for the social skill of most ordinary pupils that they learn to play the very sophisticated role of the miscreant so perceptively.

## Role maintenance function

Our study of the miscreant role offers an insight into the punishment system of the school. It is a curious feature of school punishments that the incidence of the offences for which they are meted out appears virtually unaffected by the punishments. Detentions, caning, the writing of lines are inflicted with monotonous regularity and little or no effect. This phenomenon becomes understandable when we consider the punishments as procedures for maintaining the role structure of the school rather than rational treatments for the elimination of the offences concerned. Teachers expect infringements of rules and expect to have to do something about infringements. What they are to do is governed by custom. The pupils meet the teachers' expectations that there will be infringements. It would in any case be idiotic to anticipate that, for instance, every pupil will always remember all his books. Pupils learn to predict the teacher's response to various infringements and even correctly anticipate variations in response according to the teacher's mood. In their turn, the pupils learn to respond in predictable ways to being apprehended. The result is a streamlined interaction sequence which is repeated over and over again in the life of every teacher and pupil. Any radical departure from the pattern produces bewilderment and pressure to return to the known ways. So it is that it may not be possible to introduce a theoretically more logical way of interacting if the weight of custom is too powerful. If there is to be a change in the interaction pattern, a rationalisation of the system of punishments, this may necessitate a major reformulation of roles such as has been attempted in some 'progressive' schools.

## Conclusion

We have seen that there are complicated behaviour patterns to be learnt by pupils if they are to cope adequately with the effects of their own intentional or accidental breaches of rules. An acceptable performance in the role of miscreant (in which all pupils appear at times) is an important factor in school success, and a poor performance contributes to failure and rejection.

# 12

## Ambiguity and conflict in the pupil role

One night Tito was driving the truck and his 'pa' was sitting beside him. It was a very warm night, so his pa's shirt was open, and he had a large growth of hair on his chest. His pa was smoking, and a spark flew from his cigarette, setting the hair on his chest on fire. Tito said, 'I saw the blaze, and I tried to put my pa out, and I ran off the road and hit a tree, and my pa died.'

Kelley (1962) records this incident, and comments on the trouble Tito had been having over school attendance. What is expected of Tito as a school pupil (regular attendance) is contrary to what is expected of Tito as a son (helping his mother to cope with the death of his father).

Most of the situations which involve pupils in uncertainty or conflict over their role are less dramatic than this instance. Let us look at some of the sources of ambiguity and strain to which pupils are exposed in their role performance.

### Lack of clarity and specificity in roles

Uncertainty may exist because the norms, though definite, have not been effectively communicated to the pupil. It is obviously impossible to specify in unambiguous detail all the expectations a school has for its pupils, and even if they could be spelled out it would take a long time for the pupils to assimilate all the details. The school rules which appear in a prospectus are a limited though interesting selection from the mass of prescriptions which are gradually unfolded to the new pupil as the weeks pass. He is not likely to read in the prospectus that running in the corridor is prohibited, but he will find this out when he or another pupil is hauled over the coals for doing that thing. The prospectus will not mention that pupils are not permitted to use the door next to headteacher's office, but other pupils or teachers will hurriedly enlighten him if he makes that mistake.

Hence every new pupil spends some time getting familiar with the rules; and to a lesser extent time must be spent getting to know the ways of every new teacher. Effective communication of norms is not to be achieved simply by carefully and systematically reducing them to a codified form. Pupils (like the rest of us) may not read rules. If they read them they may not take them in. Just as a good transport authority takes a great deal of trouble to indicate which way to turn at the precise moment when the traveller needs (or wants) to know, and in the place where he is likely to look for the information, so a school needs to take trouble to offer instructions at the moment when they are needed and in the form in which they are expected – which will vary with the kind of rule and the kind of pupil. It is useless to brief students on examination rules several months before they sit the examination; it is equally useless to say you wanted inch margins after some pupils have left half-inch margins.

A great deal of communication of norms is done by publicly denouncing someone who has broken a rule he did not know about. This may be effective for those who do not happen to have broken the rule, but it leaves the pupil who is denounced feeling that he has been unjustly treated.

Some rules are so general as not to constitute an effective guide to behaviour. A headteacher stated that he had no 'rules' in his school but instead pupils were expected to use their common sense. Pupils attempting to do this are likely to find that they are expected to conform to the teacher's common sense rather than their own. When they find out by trial and error what counts as common sense, then they will operate in terms of a set of rules which are no less real for the headteacher's denial that they exist.

The substitution of 'common sense' for rules has, however, some justification. It is manifestly impossible to foresee all the rules which might be necessary, as the housekeeper of a small student hostel ruefully remarked on finding that the rolling pin was covered with dents from having been used to crack walnuts. And it is sometimes unwise to state a rule which, by being stated, might suggest nefarious behaviour. Rules prohibiting the use of drugs or the sale of contraceptives by pupils would come into this class.

Learning a role in any case implies, as the headteacher no doubt wished to emphasise, not so much learning specific behaviours for every situation in which the pupil may find himself; it rather implies learning a repertoire of appropriate behaviours, and learning to select from the repertoire as the occasion demands. Reliance on specific rules too often leaves a pupil without guidance in new situations.

Even when roles have been learnt they have continually to be re-learnt as pupils grow older. At eighteen a grammar school pupil can and should behave less deferentially to his teachers than a thirteen-year-old, and must take more responsibility for his actions. He is less likely to get away with a claim that he did not know what he was supposed to do, and less easily excused for forgetting his books.

Other changes besides increasing age introduce new requirements. As a member of a school team a pupil may have to dress differently. As a club member he may be entitled to be in a room forbidden to other pupils. Whenever different norms apply to pupils according to their category, the pupil needs to be clear not only about the norms themselves but

III

also about his own category. Is he 'absent' when he spends the afternoon in the sickroom, or when he has permission to leave half an hour before the end of school? Is today a 'wet' day which would bring into force certain rules which do not operate on fine days?

Problems of transition from one category to another may impose strain on pupils. Each new beginning, at preschool, primary school, secondary school and college or university, produces symptoms of anxiety in some pupils, and orientation or briefing periods may be needed to help them cope.

A more general source of uncertainty about norms is to be found in cultural diversity. Pupils become aware that standards vary. It may be that their friends at a neighbouring school have no homework and no detentions, and call their teachers by their Christian names. Knowing this undermines commitment to the norms of their own school, making them seem after all not so mandatory. Although it is often supposed that a community with a rich diversity of norms enables more people to find ways of expressing themselves fully, in fact the effect of awareness of alternative norms is often to decrease commitment to any set of norms rather than to provide valuable options. This leads to the state of social malaise known as anomy, a normlessness which produces symptoms such as confusion and loss of identity.

## Role conflict

Norms which are ambiguous or unclear thus interfere with satisfactory role performance. Another important source of difficulty is to be found in the state of affairs exemplified in our opening quotation and known as role conflict. This involves discrepancies between norms: between norms that are part of a single role, or between norms belonging to different roles performed by the same person. We shall consider first some kinds of discrepancy which can arise within a single role.

112

Some conflicting demands within the teacher role have received comment from writers, and these have their counterpart in pupil role conflict. Teachers are, for instance, often aware of a conflict between the behaviour prescribed for professional advancement (for instance, moving from job to job for promotion) and the behaviour dictated by commitment to the needs of their pupils (Grace, 1972). We might expect pupils to experience a similar conflict between the requirement for maximum achievement and for commitment to their subjects of study. Maximum achievement results from concentrating on what is examinable and likely to be asked, whereas commitment to a subject involves grappling with points that are not clear, and exploring interesting facets, even if the knowledge so gained is unmeasurable or unlikely to be measured.

Incompatible norms within a role can often co-exist without causing strain, especially if they are not activated simultaneously. For instance, pupils are sometimes expected to do exactly as they are told, and sometimes they are expected to use judgment and think for themselves; sometimes they must copy exactly a given form, and sometimes they must be original; sometimes they are to be polite and sometimes they are to tell the truth. In such cases there need be no problem as long as there is no uncertainty about which of the conflicting norms applies in each successive situation. Difficulties arise only if the rules are generalised beyond the situation they are meant to cover. For a history essay ideas must be taken from books, and for a literary composition they must be the pupil's own ideas.

As well as distinguishing the classes of situations in which conflicting norms apply, a pupil orders the principles which govern his behaviour so that certain principles take priority in case of conflict. Telling the truth is fine as long as it does not conflict with loyalty to one's classmates, but loyalty comes first if the teacher asks him who passed him that note. Politeness comes before honesty if pupils are invited to give their opinions of teachers to teachers.

We have been discussing mainly cases of conflict between norms that are fairly generally accepted as part of the pupil role. There are other norms which vary depending on whether we consult one group of participants or another group. Pupils' classroom behaviour is governed, for instance, on the one hand by the official norms of the school as propagated by the teacher, and on the other hand by pupil peer-group norms. Although there will be many points of agreement between the two codes of behaviour, there will also be points where they disagree, as we noted in the chapter on the pupil peer group. Hence pupils are exposed to conflicting expectations: teachers may press for outstanding work, while classmates may disapprove; teachers may ban copying from others, while classmates expect it; teachers may uphold standards for hair styles and dress lengths which are rejected by pupils.

This kind of conflict seems inevitable in an institution such as the school, and it may not be harmful, if a suitable balance can be struck between fanatical enforcement of rigid prescriptions by teachers and a complete takeover by pupils. A suitable balance involves formulating official rules which are not too far out of line with developments outside the school, and particularly with the youth culture; and evolving a system of detection and penalties which seems fair to both pupils and teachers and which does not absorb too much of the energy that should be saved for teaching and learning. The aim of the arrangements for detecting and penalising breaches of official norms is often to keep infringements within bounds rather than to stamp them out; and sometimes the aim is simply to satisfy the school's public that the school is attending to its task as a guardian of standards.

In any case the school has to recognise that for many pupils the approval of their mates is more powerful than the threat of quite severe punishment, and it would be unwise to try to undermine the pupils' concern to be accepted by their peers. Socialisation involves being sensitive to the expec-

114

tations of one's fellows and taking them into account, and a pupil needs to come to terms with the society of his peers. The school may more sensibly seek to change the norms of the pupil peer group than persuade pupils to disregard them.

The expectations parents have for their children as pupils give rise to further possibilities of conflict between norms. Parents may expect a preschool child to learn to count while his teachers expect no such thing. Parents may expect homework that is against the school's policy, or disagree with the school about detentions or corporal punishment. Children are usually aware of some differences between school and parental norms. One method they can use to come to terms with conflicting sets of norms is to adopt parts from each set of norms (Lacey, 1970). For instance, they may settle for parental norms for speech, peer group norms for dress, and teacher norms for methods of working out arithmetic problems.

At times pupils may find that teachers disagree amongst themselves about what they expect, or that one teacher imposes requirements which cannot be met without disregarding another teacher's requirements. If the pupil finishes his English homework, for example, it may be at the expense of his mathematics. Or one teacher may authorise an action for which a pupil is subsequently punished by another teacher. This kind of conflict is likely to produce indignation and resentment in pupils who try to do what they are supposed to, and it is also likely to be used as an excuse for not doing what they are supposed to by less conscientious pupils who play off one authority against another.

### Conflict between roles

The discrepancies we have been considering between the various demands made on pupils in their role as pupils give rise to problems of *intra-role* conflict. A further set of problems arises from the fact that pupils, like other people, occupy a number of positions simultaneously. Conflict between the norms for different positions is *inter-role* conflict. The most significant other position which a pupil occupies is that of family member. Loyalty to the family may require a child to neglect his school work at times in order to help at home, or to use grammar and pronunciation that is frowned on by the school. Parents may desire a child to do shopping errands at lunch time or after school and the school may forbid this. Parents may allow their child more independence than the school is willing to concede.

There is extensive evidence that middle-class homes impose demands on children which fit well with those of the school. They set standards of neatness, deference to elders, conformity to rules, punctuality, aspiration and effort which agree closely with the school's prescriptions. Working-class parents, on the other hand, have an outlook that is in some ways alien to that of the school. They may approve of keeping rules in order to keep out of trouble, but they do not value neatness, punctuality, and politeness for their own sake, and school subjects often appear irrelevant to them.

Even for middle-class children, however, some conflicts occur. Important family occasions disrupt homework schedules. Sickness of a family member requires a child to undertake duties at home which interfere with his school obligations. The parents may disapprove of some of the school's policies or the teacher's actions, such as keeping children after school when the parents wanted them to be at a music lesson, or inflicting corporal punishment. Parents may wish a child to withdraw from religious observance or cadet training whereas the child is acutely aware that this will make him unpopular.

In all these cases the pupil's loyalties are divided. Some conflict between home and school norms is healthy. It helps the child to learn that neither parents nor teachers are infallible as models; the child must reconcile the conflicting demands, and this involves initiative and responsibility. But if two such important institutions as the home and the school

116

make demands that are hard to reconcile, and compete strenu-
ously for the child's allegiance, penalising him severely for
failure to conform, his attempts to reconcile his roles will be
painful and disturbing. It is better if home and school can
recognise the tension between the child's role as family member and his role as school pupil, and respect his efforts to
resolve the conflict.

Attempts to resolve such a conflict are likely to have very
serious consequences for working-class children of high ability.
They may find themselves in a school or class peopled mainly
by middle-class children. For most children it is more important to belong in a family than to belong in a school, but the
school puts powerful pressure on these children to take over
attitudes, speech and behaviour that alienate them from their
families. Some few children may be able to move between the
worlds of home and school, alternating their attitudes, speech
and behaviour, much as a competent player switches from
tennis to badminton and back. But most cannot attempt this
without coming to feel detached from at least one of their
worlds. The school might best serve its working-class pupils
by, for instance, supporting them instead of punishing them
when they stay away from school to help a sick mother, or
by helping them to make effective use of their natural language forms rather than requiring them to substitute other
forms which by historical accident have won temporary
prestige.

If the child's role as family member is at times incompatible
with his role as pupil, the role of parent is much less compatible still with the role of school pupil. But the upward
extension of secondary education and the downward extension of the age of parenthood combine to produce large
numbers of parents in the secondary school age-range. Because
we think of the role of parent as incompatible with that of
school pupil, impending parenthood is likely to end a girl's
school career and sometimes a boy's school career. Any
education offered to pregnant girls of secondary school age

117

tends to be in special institutions. Attempts are made to reconcile parental and pupil roles at the tertiary level, but the secondary level shows as yet little modification in this direction.

### Uncongenial roles

Distinct from both intra-role conflict and inter-role conflict is another kind of problem that arises in role performance when the pupil's personality or physical characteristics prevent his proper performance of the role assigned to him. The shy child obliged to display his work to the class may suffer agonies. The child who has a bright manner and 'seems' intelligent, although actually lacking ability, cannot meet his teacher's expectations. The pupil who matures early may be expected to perform and behave at a level for which he is not equipped by intellect and experience, and the late maturer may be treated as a child in spite of his experience and competence. Any child who is far from average in important school abilities is in danger of finding himself cast in a role which does not fit, and some prescriptions for pupil behaviour are at odds with general characteristics of children. For instance, it is very hard for healthy children to keep still and quiet for long periods, and any norm that requires this will be difficult to enforce.

### Ideals and actualities

Sometimes the discrepancy is not so much between the school's actual standards and the pupil's actual ability to perform, but between the pupil's perception or internalisation of the school's standards and his own ability. Some very able pupils constantly experience stress because they fall short of an impossible ideal, although their teachers are well pleased with their work.

Just as it is important to recognise the possibility of discrepancies between actual expectations and the perceptions individuals have of these expectations, so it is also important to note that there may be discrepancies between actual and ideal norms. When a rule states that pupils 'must' or 'will' at all times comport themselves with dignity when using public transport, this states an ideal which nobody expects to be achieved; minor but clear-cut departures from dignified behaviour neither occasion surprise nor attract penalties. A norm is stated in terms which come nearer to actual expectations when it introduces some such word as 'reasonable': pupils are expected to be 'reasonably' quiet on buses. It seems that requirements can be sorted into ideal standards which nobody expects to bear a close relation to what actually happens, and practical standards which are influenced by realistic appraisal of what is likely to be achieved.

## Coping with conflict

Having considered a variety of kinds of ambiguity and conflict of norms, let us now turn our attention to ways of dealing with ambiguity and conflict.

It would be a mistake to suppose that incompatible role expectations always give rise to difficulties in the mind of the pupil. In the case of teachers, it has been found (Grace, 1972) that whereas nearly two-thirds of a sample of teachers *perceived* problems in reconciling role commitment and career aspirations, only about one-quarter claimed personal experience of conflict. Similarly, although we may suspect that numbers of pupils would agree that at times they cannot please both parents and teachers, relatively few would report distress on this account. A partial explanation of the failure of objectively conflict-laden situations to produce stress is to be found in this statement by Urry (1970):

Actors do not simply internalize abstract norms in a vacuum, but images of themselves in concrete relationships

119

with specific actors or groups. A principle may only be abstracted after the specific process of rôle-taking and internalization.

This suggests that conflicting principles could be apparent to the observer, while the actor himself might be unaware of the principles and aware only of acting in accordance with a specific norm: a pupil might, for instance, follow the example of his classmates in copying homework from the class 'brain' without relating this to cheating.

Conflict, then, is not always stressful. Moreover, it may even be seen as stimulating. Grace (1972) reports that some teachers find it so: 'this is an aspect of the job which adds to its interest'. Probably some pupils also enjoy conflict. However, smooth and comfortable social interaction requires that ambiguities and discrepancies between expectations should be kept at a modest level. Role prescriptions need to be reasonably clear, specific and compatible, effectively understood by pupils, and harmonious with their capabilities. When these conditions exist, interaction can go on without unintended 'incidents'. But role prescriptions which are too complete and comprehensive have the effect of reducing the scope for individual style in role performance, emphasising the routine aspects of interaction, and reducing the impact of person on person. Occasions completely governed by detailed role prescriptions are often experienced as artificial, keeping people at a distance from one another and restricting expression of their 'real selves'; or they may be simply boring.

There are other reasons for tolerating a certain level of role ambiguity and conflict. Conflicting norms may offer alternatives which give pupils an opportunity to choose, and may also open up possibilities of change which could improve schools as institutions. One pupil who interprets mufti to permit bare feet, when the teachers had not intended this, may be paving the way for reforms in pupil attire.

Experience of stressful role conflict leads to attempts to

lessen conflict by various means. Sometimes this can be done simply by clarifying which of a number of possible definitions of the situation is to be applied. Within the classroom a change in the teacher's tone of voice and stance can clearly signal a switch from norms suitable for teacher-as-friend to norms suitable for teacher-as-boss. Geographical separation between home and school helps to establish boundaries for the jurisdiction of different sets of norms. School uniform helps to specify which set of norms is relevant by symbolising that the wearer is, while in uniform, acting in the role of pupil. Taking off the uniform, the pupil reverts to a non-pupil role, and puts aside the speech and behaviour belonging to him as a pupil. In the school precincts, moving from classroom to classroom or to the playground signals changes in expected behaviour.

Sometimes role conflict can be dealt with by separating out one or more of the components of the teacher or the pupil role. If pupils cannot reconcile teacher-as-critic with teacher-as-confidant, this difficulty could be dealt with by providing school counsellors who are not subject teachers. Pupils attracted both by the obedient-pupil role and the wicked-pupil role may sort themselves into two specialist groups, each making use of the other as a foil.

## Adaptations to conflict

When conflict cannot be resolved by manipulation of roles, pupils have to adapt to it. Merton presented a framework for examining adaptation to role conflict, and his scheme has been discussed and modified by later writers (see, for instance, Cohen, 1966). Merton was concerned with disjunction between prescribed goals and the institutionalised means of attaining those goals, a disjunction which is very important in the school setting. The school prescribes for its pupils goals of academic achievement which, as we have seen, are beyond the reach of many pupils. Some of the goals have built into them the understanding that many or most pupils cannot reach them; for example, competitive examinations are so arranged that many pupils must fail. Pupils with a favourable home background, innate capacity and good teachers have the means to reach the goal, while others who lack these advantages are denied any legitimate means of reaching the goal that is set up. Merton's scheme sets out possible responses to this situation.

Lacking the means to succeed, a pupil might, in terms of this scheme, keep striving for the goals but try to reach them by irregular means; or he might 'play along' by carrying out the prescribed actions in a perfunctory sort of way without genuinely adopting the goals; or he might abandon both goals and means and withdraw from the situation; or he might adopt the role of reformer and set to work to change both goals and means. There are other possibilities, but we need not consider them all here.

The first of these alternatives is common in schools. Pupils who want to do well but fear they may fail resort to copying someone else's work, or they lift passages from books. More extreme attempts to succeed by illegitimate means include getting another person to take their place in an examination or getting information about the questions in advance. From a practical point of view it is important to realise that such forms of deviant behaviour may be a result of commitment or indeed over-commitment to the accepted goals, and therefore require quite a different approach from deviant behaviour which involves rejection of socially approved goals. It may be more appropriate to ensure access to the means of success, or to modify the pupil's aspirations, than simply to punish him. A clear case for this approach is the situation where university students, desperate to get access to reference material which is in short supply, steal, hide or mutilate books and journals.

The second alternative, that of mere outward observance of requirements, is also very common in schools. When school

122

attendance is compulsory because the state or his parents insist, a pupil who has given up hope of gaining qualifications often settles for just getting by with a minimum of effort and keeping out of trouble. He is carrying out the rituals of classroom life without accepting the aims of the school. The readiness of many pupils to comply outwardly disguises the failure of the school to meet their needs.

The third alternative, withdrawal, is also a familiar feature of the school scene. Drop-outs have obviously abandoned both goals and means. So also have some pupils who remain at school. Although physically present they have no commitment to the school's goals and do not carry out the prescribed work. At times they substitute other goals of their own and they make use of the school to further these unofficial goals. They may, for instance, set out to 'have a giggle', that is, to extract as much fun from school life as they can (Hargreaves, 1967).

Amongst pupils, would-be reformers do not usually have much scope, so not many pupils belong in this category. Potential reformers are often forced to withdraw, or suppressed until they outwardly conform. But a few, like the writers of *Letter to a Teacher* (Barbiana, 1970), do strike a blow for the brave new world of their vision.

The responses we have been discussing could in point of fact be made even when there is no discrepancy between the goals set up by the schools and the possibility of attaining the goals in approved ways: even a capable pupil with everything going for him may discard the educational aims of the school or set up as a reformer. But there is no doubt that pupils who cannot pass examinations or gain qualifications are more likely to respond in at least some of the ways Merton described:

A boy who does badly academically is predisposed to criticise, reject or even sabotage the system where he can, since it places him in an inferior position (Lacey, 1970).

123

In extreme cases, Lacey says, such a boy may adopt values which are diametrically opposed to those of the school:

> All the people where I live say I am growing up to be a 'Ted' so I try to please them by acting as much like one as I possibly can ... I would much rather be a hooligan and get some fun out of life than be a snob always being the dear little nice boy doing what he is told.

Psychologically such an adaptation may be more healthy than acceptance of the school's judgment that the pupil is unworthy. Survival in the classroom or outside it depends on maintaining some sort of integrity as a person. If it is impossible to pass the examination or to please the teacher it may be necessary for the pupil to reject the teacher's values in order to retain his own self-respect. It is hard to over-estimate the extent to which lack of congruence between the school's standards and the practicability of reaching them undermines the efforts of pupils.

To reduce the disjunction between goals and means in the school, the school can start from either end. It can adjust the goals so that each pupil is aiming at a standard he can realistically hope to reach, which is the aim of individualised instruction. Or it can try to remove obstacles thought to prevent some pupils from reaching the goals; it can take steps to counteract the effects of so-called cultural deprivation, for instance.

The concept of cultural deprivation, however, deserves further comment at this point. If we think in terms of value systems we cannot escape the conclusion that the 'culturally deprived' child fails at school not primarily because he has too little access to the knowledge held desirable by the school, but because he does not value this knowledge. It is not that his home has not magazines in it, but that he does not care about magazines. If we filled his home with magazines we might find them being used as pot-stands or spills for lighting cigarettes or toilet paper. His and his family's lack of enthusiasm for book knowledge is just one bit of a life style

124

that makes him a misfit at school. With different goals and standards, different speech and manners, he cannot share the teacher's definition of the situation and cannot meet the teacher's demands. We are dealing essentially with a normative problem, and 'cultural deprivation' is a misnomer. The cure, if there is one, involves either changing the teacher's definition of the situation or changing the pupil's value system, and tampering with value systems is a very tricky business, quite different from plugging gaps in a child's background. Perhaps it is well that the school is very inept at changing value systems.

Finally, it is worthy of note that teachers and pupils need not have the same definitions of situations provided their different definitions are compatible. The teacher may be saying 'I am paid to get these pupils through their examination', or 'Every child has a right to be exposed to the great literature of the English language', while the pupil is saying 'I want the teacher to think I'm a good guy', or 'It's best to keep out of trouble if I can'. These are compatible attitudes and may enable a class to function satisfactorily.

## Conclusion

We have seen that the role of the pupil is often unclear, and that the norms which comprise the role often conflict with each other or with the norms of other roles belonging to the pupil. We have recognised that role conflict has its uses but can also interfere with the functioning of the school and produce stress in pupils exposed to too much of it. We have noted some common responses to situations involving conflict, ways of surviving in the face of demands that run counter to one another or to the personality of the pupil.

# 13

## Role theory and the classroom

Role theory involves a set of concepts we have been using to try to describe and explain pupil behaviour. There are of course many other sets of concepts which can also be used for this same purpose – for example, interaction analysis, reference group theory, alienation, systems analysis. Each of these can lead to useful insights when applied to educational settings and each has its own special contribution to make. So it may be a good idea to try to set down the special contribution of role theory to an understanding of educational processes.

But before we do this it is as well to note that in talking in terms of roles we are using an analogy—indeed it is hard to deal in abstract ideas without finding ourselves using analogies. It is therefore important to recognise that our analogy is a less than perfect replica of the reality it is intended to represent. Some of the implications of the analogy must be rejected.

### Defects in the role analogy

In the first place, the analogy suggests something unreal about role performance : it suggests that in performing roles people are somehow not being themselves. While this is occasionally true, especially when we are new to a role as is a pupil on his first day at school, it much more often happens that our roles are truly part of us, and we are quite unaware of any detachment between ourselves and our role behaviour. Particularly is this so for ascribed roles based on sex, age, place in family and similar characteristics. In the role of father a man is not merely acting a part like the actor on the stage. He *is* father. Even occupational roles, which we might expect to be able to take on or put aside quite freely, often become part of our personality. The teacher indeed becomes dogmatic, the accountant finicky, and the salesman plausible – this is an occupational hazard. Longstanding roles become 'second nature'. So in using the role analogy we reject the implication that we are somehow pretending when we perform a role.

Another defect in the role analogy is the suggestion it conveys that our parts are clear-cut. There is often much less consensus in the details of role prescriptions than the analogy might lead us to expect. Whereas the playwright provides his characters with the lines to be spoken and the movements to be made, social roles usually prescribe only principles and guidelines, which we incorporate into a practised repertoire of behaviours. Each new situation requires us to make a fresh application of the guidelines by selecting an appropriate response from our repertoire.

Thirdly, the role analogy has a tendency to make us think too concretely about behavioural expectations. We can easily begin to think of a role as if it were something 'out there' instead of being simply an idea which helps us to conceptualise, to think about behaviour.

Having sounded a warning about misleading implications, let us now look at some of the valuable insights to be derived from the application of role theory to school situations.

*Some implications of role theory*

The existence of schools depends on substantial agreement between teachers, pupils, parents and others in their interpretation of events in classroom and other school settings. These shared interpretations or 'definitions of the situation' give rise to expectations for the behaviour of those who enter into the situations, and thus roles emerge. These roles are tied to positions in the school, positions such as pupil, teacher, prefect, or headteacher. Thus the roles reflect the functions the school is expected to perform, and the structure corresponding to those functions.

In terms of role theory, behaviour consists not of isolated acts but of sequences which fit into a few general patterns, the patterns themselves being linked into institutions and thus into the social system. 'Teacher' and 'pupil' refer to roles which apply, with variations in detail, to countless situations in different times and places.

It follows from this inter-relatedness of behavioural acts that attempts to change behaviour piece by piece, without reference to underlying definitions and role perceptions, may be a waste of effort. As an example, a teacher trying to get a class of girls keen about mathematics may be hampered by underlying unfavourable interpretations of the significance of the subject for the pupil: 'Girls are no good at mathematics – it is unfeminine'; 'What use will this be to me anyway when I leave school and work in Woolworths?' 'The other girls will think I'm mad if I say I like maths'. The would-be reformer has either to change mathematics into something that does not conflict with the pupils' definition of what is feminine, useful, or 'with-it'; or to find a way of changing the pupils' definition.

On the other hand, the very inter-relatedness of behavioural acts means that there will be times when a comparatively minor change in one norm may trigger changes in many other norms. For instance, a simple new rule that pupils are to have their midday meal at school may directly or indirectly affect the length of the lunch-hour, the attitudes of pupils towards certain foods, their table manners, the informal contacts between pupils and staff, participation of pupils in extra-curricular activities, teachers' lunch-hour supervision duties, the hours of work of working mothers, and the income of the family. Again, a general social change can bring about changes in specific norms: an increasingly affluent society may produce pupils who write on one side of the paper only, schools with car-parks, and school uniforms with a special version for summer and winter.

Some of the consequences of changes in norms or roles are likely to be unintended, as when a rule that boys' hair must not reach to their collars led boys to avoid washing their hair since it hung down further when washed. The inter-relatedness of norms, then, gives us both the possibility of using one change to produce a different change and the danger of finding that a change has produced unwanted side effects.

Agreed definitions-of-situations imply an adequate communication system. Schools generally pay very little attention to the effectiveness of communication of norms. In so far as they do consider the matter they are likely to think in terms of teachers making their expectations clear to pupils, but it is also necessary for pupils to be able to express their expectations to their teachers, and machinery to help them do this may be needed. The teacher, being older, more experienced and better able to command the support of the establishment, may often have more influence than the pupils in defining roles, but the pupils have numbers on their side, and, by failing to conform to some of the teacher's expectations, they influence the pupil role far more than is often realised.

When roles have been worked out to the satisfaction of both teacher and pupils, enjoyment is enhanced and disruption minimised. Pupils rarely or never, according to Grace (1972), challenge the successful teacher, because he manages to establish norms that are accepted as suitable and come to be taken for granted. Non-conforming behaviour is seen by the pupils themselves as inappropriate in the presence of such a teacher. If defiance does occur it is controlled and spasmodic because it is seen by the class as out-of-place.

In everyday situations it is easy to underestimate the extent to which we are influenced by shared definitions-of-situations which we never question. Most of the time we internalise the expectations of others so successfully that we are unaware of any pressure to conform. The power of the norms becomes apparent, however, when we unintentionally deviate – as the teacher who forgets to zip his fly or the choir member who makes a wrong entry or the pupil who says 'pheasants' for 'peasants' can miserably testify. We conform to the vast majority of norms without anyone specifically enforcing them, just because we feel comfortable when we conform. This tendency is rooted in the social nature of man; perhaps it is what we mean when we say that man is a social being.

Grace's picture of the classroom with the taken-for-granted norms resembles, then, the majority of social settings in our lives. But general conformity with norms makes deviant behaviour the more conspicuous, and it is a fact that deviant behaviour is very common in schools. Role theory, as we saw in Chapter 10, helps us to understand some important sources of deviant behaviour. It reveals that some forms of deviant behaviour serve a useful purpose. And it suggests methods of control for undesirable forms of deviant behaviour through changes in role definitions or through the provision of alternative roles.

Role theory has also an important contribution to make to our understanding of pupil behaviour through the concept of role conflict, which we explored in Chapter 12. In that chapter we saw that conflict may arise from the existence of competing value systems as well as from superficial inconsistencies in norms, and we took account of some of the consequences of role conflict for individual adjustment.

Talk of control of deviance and of role conflict tends to over-emphasise the restrictions roles place upon us. Some people see norms as limiting their personal freedom. The truth is that the existence of agreed patterns of behaviour enormously extends the range of activities available for human beings. Language, for instance, consists of a very elaborate set of conventions to which we must conform if we wish to be understood. But by conforming we gain access to the experience of others and to a measure of control over our environment which would be quite impossible without language. Other sets of norms perform a similar function. At the very least they serve society much as habits serve the individual. They save us the necessity of constantly making decisions about what to say, what to eat, where to sit, when to dress and what to wear – decisions which, if we had no precedent, would use so much mental energy that we would have none left to cope with the novel elements in situations. The pupil who knows where to sit, how to head up his paper, what to do if he runs out of ink, when to ask for help and how to address the teacher is in a position to concentrate on the exercise in hand.

An insight into the function of norms in extending the scope of behaviour and economising on effort may help people to accept occasional frustration when their inclinations run counter to the norms. But there will also be an inevitable tendency for norms to persist when there is good reason to redefine situations, and to overcome this tendency there is a need for flexibility in adherence to established norms. Roles are in fact being continually remodelled in response to changing circumstances and varying personal interpretations.

*Role making*

Bearing in mind this need for innovation in the shaping of roles, we see that the school as a socialising institution has a twofold function: it provides for role learning on the one hand and for role making on the other hand. This twofold function has a parallel in the school's task in relation to knowledge: the school must conserve accumulated knowledge and also make new knowledge available. Postman and Weingartner (1969) convey a similar message in their insistence that pupils should not merely receive the meanings their teachers propose but should make their own meanings out of the experience their teachers provide.

It does not make sense to ask whether the school should be conservative or innovative, whether it should teach pupils the old roles or help them forge new roles. Surely it must do both. The question is only, how much of each?

If we are concerned mainly that existing roles should be well-learnt, pupils will be expected to accept the models proposed by their teachers. But if we want schools to foster a creative process also, role-making becomes a continuing task for pupils and teachers together, and the outcome cannot be set down in advance. We cannot say to our pupils, 'Be original: do this'.

# 14

## Change

We have been discussing the role of the pupil as it is found in typical schools of today. Some of our examples have even come from past decades, since many features of today's schools have come to us more or less unchanged from the past. But changes which are in evidence in a small proportion of schools require us to qualify some of our generalisations, and we are likely to see accelerated change in the rest of this century. It is now time to examine some of the trends which are modifying the role of the pupil and will so change this role that it may soon have little in common with the role we have been discussing.

### Children's liberation

One of the background forces at work to change the role of the pupil is a children's rights movement which has some points in common with other human rights movements such as women's liberation. A number of independent pressures in the direction of greater autonomy for the young can be seen as reinforcing each other to strengthen children's rights. Young people now more often marry and more often become parents before the traditional age of majority. There is a move to extend the voting age downwards. Wages at the beginning of the young person's working life, and bursaries for higher education, offer better prospects of economic independence than before, and a rising tide of affluence has freed the young generation from the fear of poverty that made their parents so anxious to succeed within the system. Adolescents leave home earlier. These practical changes are backed by a philosophy which questions the right of parents to prescribe a way of life for their own children: even to inflict on their children penalties for having inadequate parents, or to reward them for having unusually competent parents. Movements like Headstart on the one hand, and pressure for the abolition of fee-paying schools on the other hand, share a common tendency to attack the influence of parents over their children's future.

Bereiter (1973) writing of the 'trend toward the extension of individual freedoms and civil rights' has this to say:

> I have suggested that the rights of children represent a new frontier in this movement – a most difficult frontier to be sure, but one that seems likely to be broached in some way. At the very least, the right of adolescents to live their lives as adolescents and not as adults in the process of formation is likely to gain some recognition.

Bereiter goes on to predict that cultural pluralism will express itself in general acceptance of the right to experiment with unusual life styles.

Even psychology and the study of child development contribute to a new view of the rights of children, proclaiming the uniqueness of each child and supporting his right to develop in his own way. In schools, new wealth and new technology combine to make possible individualised instruction which tries to fit the teaching to the child instead of trying to induce the child to adjust to the teaching. Together, trends such as these are having a profound effect on the role of the child and the role of the pupil, although Katkin (Gottlieb, 1973) can still assert that 'We seem unable to

134

respond to our youngsters both as children with special needs and as people with equal rights.'

The school has been considered by some writers to be a subtle and even sinister way of denying rights to children. As an institution it has too many of the features of total institutions as described by Goffman (1968) for us to feel comfortable about it: its pupils are captives, largely segregated from the rest of the world over a long period of years, bureaucratically managed, made to subordinate themselves to the staff, supervised constantly to ensure compliance. The demands of the school pursue pupils into the streets beyond the school and into their homes, through school uniform requirements and homework, and onto the playing field in their hours of recreation through required participation in school teams. The school as an institution is engaged in an attempt to make over the personalities of its pupils, much as prisons and mental hospitals attempt to make over the personalities of their inmates. And the school has at hand much more potent instruments for making over personalities than ever before, such as behaviour modification techniques, counselling, and a variety of encounter group procedures. Some protection from unfair exposure to such techniques may be needed:

> The old techniques of coercion and indoctrination could be justifiably banned or restricted. The new ones are not in themselves encroachments on individual liberty and they have potential for giving individuals what they want. Thus it will make no sense to suppress them. Protection for the individual will require that such techniques not be imposed without his competent consent (Bereiter, 1973).

We send children to school sincerely believing it to be very much for their own good, but it seems that we have to deny them freedom in order to 'school' them; and if we ever come to doubt (like Illich, 1971) that it is to their

135

advantage to be 'schooled', then there is no longer any excuse for this denial of freedom.

## Access to the real world

However, we may tackle this problem by trying to change the schools so that they cater better for children's liberation, instead of throwing away the schools as Illich would have us do. One way to make the schools less constricting may be to break down the barriers between the school and the world outside the school. We may advocate bringing the community into the school through parent participation and the involvement of outside individuals and agencies; or we may opt for taking the school into the community through factory visits, nature walks, class camps, excursions to France, work experience and the like. Developments of this kind can be seen not only as breaking down the walls which shut children up in schools, but also as increasing the reality component in education. Toffler (1970) points out that the ratio of vicarious to real experience has been increasing rapidly in the modern world. The school is par excellence the purveyor of vicarious experience. It exists so that the child may take a short cut from the primitive wisdom of the infant to the accumulated wisdom of society, by-passing the slow stages by which man has laboured over thousands of years to understand and master his environment. In spite of 'discovery methods', the school basically passes on what others have discovered. New media – films, tapes, television – seem to make subjects more 'real' but in fact only increase the range and vividness of vicarious experience. One sees Bangkok without smelling it or sweating in its heat. Even the visit to Paris, which seems to have taken the pupil into the real world at last, still leaves him in the role of an onlooker, a role of minimum involvement. Thus something more radical than visits by pupils is needed if schools are to be truly integrated into society; an integration of *goals and processes* rather than settings. If

136

the pupil in the school has a goal that is rooted in the world beyond, and uses processes that are genuine in terms of that world, then the fact that he does this in a classroom may not constitute a barrier between him and the world. The pupil who wants to use a computer can work his way through a programmed text on computer language in a school classroom without feeling that the school is out of touch with reality.

## The place of the adolescent

One aspect of the rights of children, then, concerns their right to become involved in the real world instead of being segregated in a specially constructed child's world. As long as schooling was mainly for the young (up to early adolescence) it appeared reasonable to construct a child's world in which adults determined for the child what he needed to know and do. This seems a less reasonable thing to do as pupils grow older, and many of the changes currently taking place in education are related to the upward extension of schooling to late adolescence. This extension coincides with a downward trend in the age of physical, intellectual and sexual maturity. Boys and girls of seventeen and eighteen are more mature than their parents were at the same age. They are capable of holding adult jobs even if the wage structure refuses them adult pay, and they are old enough to marry and have children. And these young people swell the ranks of pupils in larger numbers year by year. This has undoubtedly contributed to the demand from pupils themselves for more autonomy, to a diminishing respect for the authority of the teacher as such, and to criticism of curricula as irrelevant. In tune with these pressures from the pupils is a trend towards replacement of the prefect system, which was an extension of the authority of the teachers downwards into the ranks of the pupils, by a system of school councils in which the pupils themselves take a hand in setting up and maintaining

137

order, and begin to press for a voice in curriculum decisions as well.

This marks a new role for the pupil. His own perception of the relevance of the school's offering to his present wants and future plans will have to be taken into account. Loyalty to his school and obedience to his teachers will be less conspicuous. Some secondary school pupils will be part-time pupils, selecting from the offerings of the school only what they want, and perhaps selecting from more than one school. These pupils, like students in adult education classes at present, and like apprentices in day-release classes, will owe primary allegiance to jobs and not to the school. They may have wives or husbands, and children. Some may be older men and women who have come back to school after some years, to develop their skills or their interests, a change that will be made possible by a new approach to the distribution of income and educational entitlement. The division that now marks off secondary from tertiary and adult education will become blurred and vanish. As secondary education or its equivalent becomes more available for adult men and women, it will be less urgent to keep adolescents at school as long as possible before they start work. The legal leaving age may be reduced or abolished.

Motherhood will cease to be an indication for the termination of secondary education, as it has largely ceased to bar women from tertiary education. This small change by itself could revolutionise some aspects of the role of senior secondary school pupils. Parents, even if they are only seventeen years old, could hardly be asked to bring notes from their mothers explaining why they were absent, nor could pregnant girls be required to wear the school uniform.

Changes in economic aspects of the status of children can be expected to change pupil roles. If adolescents cannot leave school till they are, say, sixteen, they are prevented from earning a living and must remain dependent on their parents, while the school holds them captive. Raising the school leaving

138

age has been in some countries in part a measure to keep young people from the labour market when jobs were scarce. In the past, dependence has continued well beyond the compulsory age of attendance at school for most adolescents, since neither beginning wages nor bursaries were sufficient to make them self-supporting. There is a trend towards an increase in bursaries, and rising affluence has made even low wages adequate to support single workers who do not aspire to high material standards of living. If, as some people have suggested, we concede the right of all our adolescents to a living income whether as a wage or a bursary or an allowance, they will become independent of their parents in deciding how long to continue their education and what sort of education to pursue. The number of unwilling pupils will dwindle, and we can surmise that courses will have to seem more relevant to the pupils' needs in order to attract customers.

## Role of the lifelong pupil

Many of the developments we have been discussing can be drawn together in the statement that what is now needed is a role for the pupil that is compatible with a great many more other roles than has previously been the case. The pupil role of the adult learner and the role of the pupil in high school, college, and university will be more alike: the pupil as customer will choose his education from a range of offerings, to suit his other concerns. The pupil role will no longer be typically a childhood role, since education is to be life-long; it will be compatible with part-time or full-time work and with running a home and raising a family. Timetables will be much more flexible, course structures freer. Most significantly, the authoritarian relationship between adult-teacher and child-pupil will no longer be dominant except in early education. The pupil may be older than the teacher. Pupils of all ages may work together, as indeed has often been the case in a more distant past. The all-age class of the present enlightened school includes children over a range of several years. The class of the future may group together children and adults over a range of a generation or more.

Adult pupils can more easily see their teachers as social equals, with limited authority in an area of special expertise. But even when the traditional age-gap between teacher and pupil is maintained, today's conditions make it difficult or impossible for the teacher to sustain the role of the knowledge expert. Not again will anyone be able to write as Goldsmith wrote of the village schoolmaster:

And still they gazed, and still the wonder grew
That one small head could carry all he knew.

The knowledge explosion has made it impossible for one person to have at his disposal real expertise in even the whole of one science, and books and the other mass media, with general literacy, have at the same time offered access to expert knowledge for all and sundry. A four-year-old may come to light with items of information not known to his teacher, and, by the time pupils are ten or twelve, there are some in every class who know more than some of their teachers about some parts of the curriculum. As long as pupils expect teachers to know more than they know themselves, they are scornful of every lapse – 'call *her* a teacher' was the comment of a country class when they found that their teacher had not known a cow had to calve in order to yield milk. It is obvious that teachers urgently need release from the daunting expectation that they will know more than their pupils.

And today's technology offers a way for teachers to relinquish their role as a prime source of knowledge. Non-human resources in the form of books, programmed texts, teaching machines, computer-aided instruction, films, tapes, and television have begun to take over from the brain of the teacher as repositories of information. As these aids are used increasingly to cope with the knowledge explosion, the function of the teacher could become something between that of a librarian, guiding pupils to appropriate source material, and counsellor, helping pupils to define their aims and to work towards them. Correspondingly the pupil will gain in independence and responsibility, and will take a more active part in learning.

At the same time the role of the teacher as assessor may recede, opening the way for greater trust and co-operation between pupil and teacher. Many of the new teaching materials have testing procedures built into them. As he learns, the pupil is given opportunities to check his grasp of information, and can judge his own progress without recourse to the teacher. This impersonal feedback is less likely to engender hostility towards the teacher, and the pupil can come to terms with his limitations without the mediation of another person who sits in judgment on him.

### The pupil's choice of values

If the teacher can no longer surpass his pupils in knowledge, doubts are also being cast on his right to prescribe for them in matters of values. Should the teacher impose his own cultural goals on children who belong to a different culture or subculture? Should working-class children be converted to middle-class values? Thus the missionary role of the teacher is also challenged and greater latitude in choice of goals is allowed to pupils as teachers become less certain they know best. It is conceded that pupils have a right to pursue their own excellence and not the excellence of the teacher. Salesgirl and caretaker, hairdresser and truck driver have their excellence which differs from the excellence of the mathematician or surgeon.

## Learning together

The most fortunate pupils in all ages have probably been those who were privileged to learn with their teachers rather than from them. In the foreword to Hogan (1970), Clegg says of Hogan that he 'became outstandingly successful by learning with those whom he was appointed to teach and to help. And this of course is the secret of all good teaching'. And Hogan himself comments: 'The most effective teaching is a transmission not of information but of interest, zest, curiosity, and enthusiasm'. This theme is repeated in *New Roles for the Learner* (Mason, 1967):

> Teachers and children together need to explore patterns of information new to both of them, and the teacher's skill as a learner is his most valuable skill.

If we accept the teacher-as-learner ideal described above, the role of the pupil is eagerly to seek out new knowledge, using his teacher as a collaborator. Pupil and teacher ideally decide together on the direction of their seeking. The pupil takes over from the teacher part of the teacher's traditional role of authority, and shares with the teacher part of his own role as learner.

## Social needs of pupils

Discussions of change in our schools have a way of focussing on the learning of knowledge and skills. Would-be reformers, it seems, generally accept the view of teachers, parents, and pupils that pupils go to school essentially to obey their teachers and learn 'subjects'. However, as our discussion of the pupil peer group suggests, schools perform a very important function in providing a setting for child society.

As an institution for meeting the social needs of adolescents

142

the high school, for all its wretchedness, is peculiarly appropriate ...

High school is a sort of coeducational work-place with hourly coffee breaks. There is nothing else quite like it. Classes provide a legitimate reason for boys and girls to congregate. Class activities provide legitimate occasions for them to interact (Bereiter, 1973).

Moreover, in school classes everyone belongs. Even the boy or girl with very low peer group status has a rightful place in the group. It is because schools meet vitally important social needs for children that alternative ways of transmitting knowledge and skills do not justify 'deschooling' society. By accident, an institution evolved to meet one purpose has become defective for that purpose but is serving another very important purpose. Schools could be made to meet the social needs of adolescents much better than they do. To eliminate schools without making provision for youthful social needs would, on the other hand, be disastrous. It may be theoretically possible to learn more efficiently in isolation, through books, television, and computer assisted programmes, but the resulting social deprivation would probably not only impoverish social life, it would also in practice conspicuously interfere with the learning of knowledge and skills. Even adults, who are less dependent on social contacts than adolescents, often choose to learn in classes and by personal contact rather than in private, finding in their class membership a stimulus and motivation essential for effective learning. It would be perilous to abandon schools merely because pupils have access to other sources of information or skill.

## Conclusion

Some of the changes we have been discussing are already beginning to take place. Many voices are raised in favour of more fundamental and widespread reform, and, if the reformers have their way, the essential result will be more freedom and more responsibility for pupils to learn what they choose to learn, and to take a much larger share in the shaping of their own role. We need not imagine that pupils will be content to accept new roles which teachers construct for them. Role making is to be an open-ended enterprise in which pupil and teacher join. As far as is compatible with the like freedom of others, pupils need freedom to create new roles, so that society can be enriched by their energy and talent.

# Further reading

The text in conjunction with the bibliography offers a number of suggestions for further reading. A few of the more useful and interesting are selected for comment here, and some additional background reading is suggested.

For those wishing to explore role theory, useful statements are to be found in M. Banton, *Roles*, Basic Books, 1965 and in B. Biddle and E. J. Thomas (eds), *Role Theory: Concepts and Research*, Wiley, 1966. A good account of role theory applied to education is to be found in D. Hargreaves, *Interpersonal Relations and Education*, Routledge & Kegan Paul, 1972.

An earlier volume in the Students Library of Education series, E. Hoyle, *The Role of the Teacher*, 1969, deals with topics which are closely related to pupil roles. Then W. Waller's *The Sociology of Teaching*, Wiley, 1965, first published in 1932, remains after more than forty years a rewarding source of insight into what goes on in schools.

Two recent accounts of school life based on extensive participant observation are essential reading for information on pupil roles: D. Hargreaves, *Social Relations in a Secondary School*, Routledge & Kegan Paul, 1967, and C. Lacey, *Hightown Grammar*, Manchester University Press, 1970. A very different document is *Letter to a Teacher*, from the School of Barbiana, Random House, 1970, a translation from the

Italian in which a group of schoolboys denounce the education system that rejected them.

Fictional accounts of the experiences of school teachers, obviously based on personal experience, are easy to read and even hilarious, while at the same time they provide vivid insights into the meaning of classroom events. Examples are listed in the bibliography under the names of E. Blishen and E. Braithwaite.

E. Goffman's books, though not written about schools, interpret everyday behaviours in ways that very often throw light on interaction between pupils and teachers. *Strategic Interaction*, University of Pennsylvania Press, 1969, *Relations in Public*, Penguin, 1972, *Interaction Ritual*, Allen Lane, 1967 and *The Presentation of Self in Everyday Life*, Doubleday, 1959 all are well worth consulting.

A useful discussion of theories of deviance can be found in A. Cohen, *Deviance and Control*, Prentice-Hall, 1966, but again this treatment does not relate specifically to the educational scene. Two articles in the Open University set book, *School and Society*, Routledge & Kegan Paul, 1971 – C. Wertham, 'Delinquents in schools' and A. Cicourel and J. Kitsuse, 'The social organization of the high school and deviant adolescent careers' – raise some interesting points. The studies by Hargreaves and Lacey already mentioned also make important contributions to the understanding of deviant behaviour in schools.

Finally, for a consideration of the future of the teacher-pupil relationship, a selection of the deschooling literature such as Ivan Illich, *Deschooling Society*, Calder & Boyars, 1971 and C. Bereiter, *Must We Educate?*, Prentice-Hall, 1973, along with A. Toffler's *Future Shock*, Bodley Head, 1970 could be read in conjunction with a much less futuristic volume edited by E. Mason, *New Roles for the Learner*, University of London Goldsmiths' College, 1967.

# Bibliography

ADAMS, R. S. (1970), 'Interaction in Classrooms' in Campbell, W. J., ed., *Scholars in Context*, Sydney: Wiley.

BARBIANA, SCHOOL OF (1970), *Letter to a Teacher* (translated Rossi, N. and Cole, T.), New York: Random House.

BEREITER, C. (1973), *Must we Educate?*, Englewood Cliffs, N. J.: Prentice-Hall.

BERNBAUM, G. (1971), 'Education, Innovation and Society. Countesthorpe: A Case Study', unpublished manuscript.

BLISHEN, E. (1966), *Roaring Boys*, London: Panther.

BLISHEN, E. (1971), *This Right Soft Lot*, London: Panther.

BOWMAN, M. J. (1968), 'The Human Investment Revolution in Economic Thought' in Blaug, M., ed., *Economics of Education 1*, Harmondsworth: Penguin.

BRAITHWAITE, E. R. (1961), *To Sir, With Love*, London: Bodley Head.

CAMPBELL, W. J., ed. (1970), *Scholars in Context*, Sydney, Wiley.

CARTER, M. (1966), *Into Work*, Harmondsworth: Penguin.

CICOUREL, A. V. and KITSUSE, J. I. (1971), 'The Social Organization of the High School and Deviant Adolescent Careers' in *School and Society*, Open University, London: Routledge & Kegan Paul.

CLARK, B. R. (1962), *Educating the Expert Society*, San Francisco: Chandler.

BIBLIOGRAPHY

CLARK, B. R. and TROW, M. A. (1965), 'College Subcultures' in Broom, L. and Selznick, P., eds, *Sociology*, New York: Harper & Row.

COHEN, A. K. (1966), *Deviance and Control*, Englewood Cliffs, N. J.: Prentice-Hall.

COMENIUS, J. A. (1632?), see Keatinge (1967).

DOUGLAS, J. W. B. (1964), *The Home and the School*, London: MacGibbon & Kee.

FLEMING, P. (1944), *The Social Psychology of Education*, London: Routledge & Kegan Paul.

FLEMING, P. (1961), 'The Man We Killed' in Inglis, B., ed., *John Bull's Schooldays*, London: Hutchinson.

FRAIBERG, S. H. (1959), *The Magic Years*, New York: Charles Scribner's Sons.

GOFFMAN, E. (1968), *Asylums*, Harmondsworth: Penguin.

GOFFMAN, E. (1969), *Strategic Interaction*, Philadelphia: University of Pennsylvania Press.

GOFFMAN, E. (1972), *Relations in Public*, Harmondsworth: Penguin.

GOTTLIEB, D., ed. (1973), *Children's Liberation*, Englewood Cliffs, N. J.: Prentice-Hall.

GRACE, G. R. (1972), *Role Conflict and the Teacher*, London: Routledge & Kegan Paul.

HARGREAVES, D. H. (1967), *Social Relations in a Secondary School*, London: Routledge & Kegan Paul.

HARGREAVES, D. H. (1972), *Interpersonal Relations and Education*, London: Routledge & Kegan Paul.

HINES, B. (1968), *A Kestrel for a Knave*, Oxford: Pergamon.

HOGAN, J. M. (1970), *Beyond the Classroom*, Reading: Educational Explorers.

HOYLE, E. (1969), *The Role of the Teacher*, London: Routledge & Kegan Paul.

HUGHES, T. (1948 ed.), *Tom Brown's Schooldays*, London: Dent (first published 1857).

148

ILLICH, IVAN D. (1971), *Deschooling Society*, London: Calder & Boyars.

INGLIS, B. ed. (1961), *John Bull's Schooldays*, London: Hutchinson.

JACKSON, P. W. (1968), *Life in Classrooms*, New York: Holt, Rinehart, Winston.

KEATINGE, M. W. (1967), *The Great Didactic of John Amos Comenius*, New York: Russell & Russell.

KELLEY, E. C. (1962), *In Defense of Youth*, Englewood Cliffs, N. J.: Prentice-Hall.

KIPLING, R. (1929), *Stalky and Co.*, London: Macmillan.

LACEY, C. (1970), *Hightown Grammar*, Manchester University Press.

LEVINSON, D. J. (1959), 'Role, Personality, and Social Structure in the Organizational Setting', *J. Abnormal and Social Psych.*, 58.

MASON, E., ed. (1967), *New Roles for the Learner*, University of London Goldsmiths' College.

MERCURIO, J. (1972), *Caning: Educational Rite and Tradition*, Syracuse University.

MINTURN, L. and LAMBERT, W. W. (1964), *Mothers of Six Cultures*, New York: Wiley.

MORRIS, B. S. (1967), 'An Outline of Normal Development' and 'Towards Mental Health in School', in Connell, W. F. *et al.*, eds, *Readings in the Foundations of Education*, London: Routledge & Kegan Paul.

MUSGRAVE, P. W. (1965), *The Sociology of Education*, London: Methuen.

MUSGROVE, F. and TAYLOR, P. H. (1969), *Society and the Teacher's Role*, London: Routledge & Kegan Paul.

NEWSOM REPORT (1963), *Half Our Future*, London: HMSO.

OPIE, I. and P. (1959), *The Lore and Language of School Children*, London: Oxford University Press.

OPIE, I. and P. (1969), *Children's Games in Street and Playground*, London: Oxford University Press.

149

## BIBLIOGRAPHY

PETERS, R. S., ed. (1969), *Perspectives on Plowden*, London: Routledge & Kegan Paul.

POSTMAN, N. and WEINGARTNER, C. (1969), *Teaching as a Subversive Activity*, London: Pitman.

ROTHNEY, J. W. M. (1968), *Methods of Studying the Individual Child*, New York: Blaisdell.

TENNYSON, ALFRED, LORD (1967), *The Works of Tennyson*, London: Macmillan.

TOFFLER, A. (1970), *Future Shock*, London: Bodley Head.

URRY, J. (1970), 'Role Analysis and the Sociological Enterprise', *Sociological Review*, 18.

VALENTINE, C. W. (1956), *The Normal Child*, Harmondsworth: Penguin.

WALLER, W. (1965), *The Sociology of Teaching*, New York: Wiley (first published 1932).

WHITING, B. B., ed. (1963), *Six Cultures*, New York: Wiley.

WILLIAMSON, H. (1961), 'Out of the Prisoning Tower' in Inglis, B., ed., *John Bull's Schooldays*, London: Hutchinson.

WILSON, B. R. (1962), 'The Teacher's Role', *British Journal of Sociology*, 13, 1.

For Product Safety Concerns and Information please contact our EU
representative GPSR@taylorandfrancis.com
Taylor & Francis Verlag GmbH, Kaufingerstraße 24, 80331 München, Germany

www.ingramcontent.com/pod-product-compliance
Lightning Source LLC
Chambersburg PA
CBHW062036270326
41929CB00014B/2449